FISICALITY

AN ANABOLIC APPROACH TO
MONEY MANAGEMENT

FISICALITY

AN ANABOLIC APPROACH TO
MONEY MANAGEMENT

CHARLES HODGE

IVT PUBLISHING

POST-PRODUCTION EDITORS

Editor-in-Chief: Charles Hodge

Senior Editor: Maxine Parker

Associate Editor: Desireé Hodge

A **BARGAIN** IS SOMETHING YOU MIGHT NOT WANT,

PROBABLY CAN'T USE, AND DEFINITELY DON'T NEED

— BUT, AT A PRICE YOU **CAN'T RESIST**.

– FRANKLIN JONES (HODGERIAN REINTERPRETATION)

CONTENTS

163 SECTION 9 INFORMATION DESK

OMNIA

EN MUNDO

EST IGNIS

ET EGO

SUM

FRIGUS

FERRO

fisicality

| ˈfi-zi-ˈka-lə-tē |
[fiz-ee-kal-i-tee]

noun

1. the concordant intermingling of fiscal and
   physical theories
   : the amalgamated fiscal and physical attributes
   of a person, act, or philosophy

2. an act or instance of financial governance using
   anabolic growth principles
   : aggressive Value Investing

3. the resultant combination of diverse financial
   matters and strength training elements that form
   a whole

4. the quality or state of being financially cock
   diesel

PREFACE

This is not a refined preface (and some may say the same about this entire book after reading it). And, I am not uniquely qualified to write a book on finances. I've made 6 figure stock trades, but I'm not rich, by modern society's grandiose standards. I'm a college dropout with 146 credit hours (too much switching majors). I only needed 2 electives to graduate, but a finance office rule change, before my last semester, stopped people with balances from registering, and I owed $3,500. But, the reason doesn't matter – I'm a dropout. I'm a failed business owner. I've bedeviled myself with credit card balances of over $60,000, for years at a time. I've been homeless, and I was in my early 40s, when I finally had an undistorted Net Worth above $0.00. I only started earnestly saving for retirement, in my mid 40s. I didn't become debt free, until my late 40s. And to keep the number 4 theme going, I've had credit scores in the 400s. I've lost money on penny stocks, the cannabis investing fad, and crypto currency. Yup, I've made lots of errors. And, I've overcome all of them. So, in some way, I guess that makes me more than qualified to write a book about what I've learned to do (and not do), based on my having made so many mistakes. However, as I remix the old yarn attributed to Thomas Edison, "I didn't actually make mistakes, but I instead simply discovered a bunch of stuff that didn't work".

No one grows or improves alone. I've had a lot of people along the way that have given me things to keep me focused on succeeding. I won't use any full names (maybe in an update, if some of them see this and say it's OK), but they'll be identified enough for them to know that I appreciate them. However, the town I'm from is also included in the list. There has never been a time someone has asked me where I was from, and I didn't say, "Henderson, N.C.". I would clear up any confusion by letting them know that any place where I was **Living**, at any time, was not where I was **From**. I was built in Henderson. But, I have taken bits and pieces from people I was fortunate enough to briefly walk through life with. I have this strange, mental quirk where time is not necessarily linear for me. The past and present are all mixed up. I feel just as strong about things that happened 45 years ago as I do things that happened 45 minutes ago. It's like the long ago thing only just actually happened, just now, for me. There's a constant mental playback of my time spent with people who are important to me, so when I see someone I haven't even spoken to in 20 years, it's like I just saw them 10 minutes ago. That interaction is usually hard for them, but always easy for me.

Pavlak is the guy who would give you opportunities and look out for you without you ever knowing he was looking out or protecting you. Once he deemed you a person of high integrity, you always had a dependable resource and reference. It was not uncommon for him to throw someone directly into a blazing fire, while also giving them a fire helmet, breathing apparatus, and directions to the exit. Once the flames were out, he'd tell them, "I knew you could do it". He was one of those decision makers with high expectations (the nature of the work demanded it), but unique in that he actually listened to the team. He would even relinquish control for certain things and implement a team member's work plan, even though he disagreed with it. This would let everybody know that his faith and confidence were in the person and not the plan. I adopted that same methodology, once I became the primary decision maker. As the manager in charge, I can always pull rank; as the leader in charge, I rarely have to.

Craig, Joe, and Jimmy were all U.S. Special Forces, Marine Force RECON and/or Navy SEAL. **Craig** used to knock the wind out of me every other day. **Jimmy** tore muscles in my lower back and hamstring. **Joe** cracked my arm and knocked out one of my molars. These were great guys. I'd train with Joe 2-4 hours and then we'd go wax philosophical at a diner for 8 hours. Joe helped get me through some rough times, for sure. I was always struck by how touchy and unsure these guys were. They were probably more easily hurt than the average person. But they were also 10 times as tough as the average person, because they could swallow those razor blades and get to work on whatever leathery task they knew they were supposed to be doing. From Joe, I learned that it was OK to be hurt, discouraged, and disgusted by something all you want, but it was NEVER OK to not do what you were supposed to be doing or honor-bound to be doing.

I had arguably the most honest, unfiltered, sincere conversations in my life with **Turek**. He was completely, totally, and utterly straight with you – on everything. You didn't have to figure out any deception with him. For a guy like me who is always looking for the stain of ethical oiliness, it was good to have a guy like him around. I reclaimed energy that was usually wasted scrutinizing delusory motivations. He is one of the most principled people I know. Heck, half of the power tools in my shed were given to me by Turek. If I was working on something and he had a spare tool that could help, he'd just bring it in and give it to me – not to borrow but to own. He didn't check before hand; he just did it. He's a throwback to a time when men who respected other men being men, also supported them being men. To this day, if I see someone in need who is right-minded and trying to do the right thing, if I can assist, I just do it.

In high school, Person, Snoody, Kittrell, Sam, and Tony were some of my cohorts. All of these guys were good-natured, intelligent, solid men – good citizens. We all had things in common. **Person** and I were both into "Morris Day and the Time", and he was always trying to cross you up, on the basketball court, with a Michael Jordan move. **Kittrell** used to like artwork, so I would pass along some of my portfolio pieces to him, from time-to-time. **Sam**, **Tony**, and I used to exchange comic books, with the "Conan: The Barbarian" ones always being a hot commodity. And, **Snoody** thought I might have been certifiably insane. I remember once, during Spanish class, he said, "I don't know what you're talking about, half the time, but I'm down with you". There are lots more folks that I could and may bring up in a more extensive recollection, but having people accept you, when your thought process is outside of the norm, is about all a fella can ask for.

    Rook, Les, Golden, and G-Worse were the guys at N.C. State that always tried to pass along knowledge. There was a time when collegiate upperclassmen would actively mentor and educate the underclassmen. Sometimes, it was just a quick word of wisdom or warning in passing, as you dapped each other up, on the yard. Other times, one of them might pull you aside and set you straight on something, while thoughtfully still respecting your manhood and individuality. **Rook** and **Les** gave no quarter, in the weight room. Les was especially unforgiving and merciless, but he also told you everything you needed to know to stay safe and healthy. I loved it. Les was the first person in college I remember talking to who was committed to the notion of people working for themselves, owning their own business, or having a dedicated side-hustle. Rook, on the other hand, was telling me way back in the late 1980s, to "buy yourself some of that computer stock with Microsoft". If only I had listened then. Sure, it wasn't as easy to buy stock then as it is now, but it could have been done. Rook guided me more than anyone and kept me out of a lot of the trouble I was sometimes prone to find myself in. **Golden** had a side gig as a photographer, and let me tell you, he was always trying to find a way to level up. He was always schooling me on how to improve myself and challenging me to try new things. He had this philosophy of not letting the things you were doing right become degraded because you were trying something new. He said you had to turn the knobs and flip the switches on everything you were into on a regular basis, so you could still use them when you needed them. **G-Worse** was unrestrained, energetic, thoughtful, and contemplative, all at the same time. He could tell you the things to watch out for and to focus on, especially the things you might have been taking for granted. He made me not overlook or disregard something that I was doing that was good or proper, just because I was used to it. I began to archive and protect my gifts more, from talking with G-Worse. These men taught me that, for those you respect and who you want to see good things go down for, you have an obligation to teach and an obligation to be taught.

Arnel and **Don** were the two technicians that trained me when I first got into Information Technology. I'm older than both of them, but I was OK with listening to them and learning from them. Too often I recall seeing older people not being able to learn, because they failed to listen to something someone younger than them was saying. Don didn't play. You couldn't fool him, and he'd check you. I remember I had built a live redundant cluster that was in Production, and he asked if it was transparent failover capable. After I said "Yes", he walked around behind it, and villainously, yanked the power cable for the Master Server out of the wall. He just yanked it out. The cluster successfully failed over, but that made it clear to me to take my work critically serious. Arnel, conversely, was more like a grade school teacher who poked you along. And aside from him showing me how to build SAN storage clusters and inspiring me to complete my training for my computer certifications, Arnel was also a very good fighter, who taught me a couple of things. I remember we once trained using a lot of Muay Thai kicks, which I am not adept at – lots of bone-to-bone contact. Afterwards was a painful, slow, limping, walk home for me. He called me after he'd gotten home saying it took him a while to figure out what was all over his pants legs. It was my skin and assorted flesh. He said it looked like curled up pork rinds. We still giggle about that one to this day.

I had gotten my Real Estate Salesperson's license in the early 1990s and was peppering cars, apartment complexes, shopping malls, and the general public with flyers for "$0.00 Down Payment HUD Homes". I thought I might be able to level up and get more callbacks, if I had money for better flyers, customer packets, and maybe even one of those newfangled cell phones. Enter Henderson, N.C.'s **Gateway Foundation**. Even with my "Best-of-Amateur-Hour Business Plan", they loaned me $2,000 to help me realize my vision. I created a corporate entity, upgraded my flyers, created customer packets, and acquired better technical gear. Then, I attempted to wear out as many pairs of shoes as I could, by doubling my Belly-to-Belly prospecting efforts. I failed miserably – wrong guy, at the wrong time, in the wrong market, with **the wrong support team**. I didn't pay the money back. I didn't have it. I had not only used up all of the loan money, but I had also depleted all of my personal reserve money (I was a full commitment, all-in kind of guy). This was damaging, not just to me, because I didn't satisfy my obligation, but also because the next person in the loan queue would be negatively impacted. I didn't refill the Gateway coffers with the money I owed, and that hurt the program. This has been one of my most bothersome, nagging failures. Because of my Gateway experience, I've subsequently helped many people, like Gateway helped me. If I run across someone trying to do good things, especially if they are inexperienced and running into roadblocks, I'll often pitch in. Sometimes, I help very little little; sometimes, I help a whole lot – but, I've given that original amount back 10x over in money, goods, services, and time. Maybe the person I help fails, or maybe they succeed; either way, I never expect anything back. And, I'm OK with that.

Sed, Dex, Dabi, Joe-Ski, Kerm, EA, Et, and Trice were my core squad, in college. All of these guys were extremely rare (as life would later prove), because they would willingly put themselves in harm's way and suffer damage, for their squad. **Sed** was always positive and had a "Can Do" attitude. If you were doubting yourself on something when Sed was in the room, by the time he left, you were ready to fight a tiger with a toothbrush. And he would stand right beside you, holding dental floss. **Joe-Ski** believed hard, and he was unflinching about it. I would label him a spiritual gangster. He was like Jeff Speakman in "The Perfect Weapon". Speakman's character wore this ring with a dragon, representing calm and wisdom, on one side and a tiger, representing, pure destruction, on the other. When he was pushed to turn the ring to the tiger side, he destroyed everything in his path. That was Joe, but his ring would be more like a lion and lamb instead. **Dex** always had your back and rather than succumb to any kind of societal pressure, would do the Right thing, when it came to his boys. If there was a hard conversation to have and information you needed to know, Dex would give it to you straight. It was not uncommon to replay the same conversation several times with Dex, as we iteratively dissected and pulled layers apart, to get to the heart of a thing. As an advisor, he was invaluable. **Dabi** was the superstar. He was Hollywood, a natural showman with amazing talent in several areas. And he was fearless. I think about the Chicago Bears' Sweetness, Walter Payton, on that run he had against the Kansas City Chiefs in 1977, where he broke ~9 tackles, in an 18-yard running back clinic. That was Dabi, always getting hit and taking an attack from some weird angle, from some weird source, absorbing it, and continuing on, stronger than ever. **Kerm** was like somebody's grand daddy who was transplanted into a young person's body. Kerm was diesel, with arms around 22". He would keep you out of trouble and make you consider the consequences of any action you were about to take, especially if it was questionable. I remember he would sometimes channel Funkadelic, when I was about to do something particularly stupid, and boom out, "You still got time to Think, Hodge; it ain't illegal, yet". And, he always wanted to see one of the fellas do good and was willing to help them get there, even if it meant him doing the dirty work behind the scenes. **EA** was an intellectual phenom. He was great to argue and debate with. His logic was always sound, so you had to bring your best material. He and I had this bright idea to start a company, probably from listening to folks like Les or Golden, that we called the Tailor Made Card Company. The idea was to hire a bunch of English majors to write custom greeting cards, and then use Art majors to design and assemble them, for our big Valentine's Day launch. We created a DBA and got to work. It didn't go well. We barely broke even. But the experience was invaluable, and I began creating what was to become my managerial approach, based on that experience. **Et** was the first person I knew that talked about owning rental property. This was while he was still a student. He talked about buying a 3-bedroom townhouse, living in 1 room, and renting out 2 rooms, to fully cover the mortgage, all the while building equity in the property. Now that I think about it, Et, Kerm, and I lived in a 3-bedroom townhouse that we rented. Hmmmm. **Trice** stands alone as probably the single toughest dude I trained with. He was slight of build but could take any kind of punishment. And he would back you up on the most dangerous predicaments you found yourself in – no hesitation, no fear, and no remorse. Dude was one of a kind. I've seen a lot of tough looking, tough talking, capable men falter and wilt, under pressure, and Trice shrugged the worst of everything off. I saw it with my own eyes. I started pulling away from all of my crew, as it grew closer to graduation time (for them, not me – college dropout, remember). My disquiet was noxious, knowing that the adventure was all almost over. I enjoyed a level of protection and affability, with those guys, that I haven't had since. I talk about all of these folks so much, that people are surprised when I tell them I haven't seen some of them in 30 years. I actually got a call from Sed not too long ago, and my first thought was something was wrong, and who do I have to go chin check, for him – unbelievable.

My first day on the job with **Simchock**, he pointed to a pile of large stone and boulders that was higher than I was tall, gave me a 12 lb. sledgehammer, and said, "Go make little ones out of big ones". By lunchtime, my cramping arms were involuntarily curling up to where I looked like a sweat-mud streaked, dusty T-Rex. I learned to be a stone mason with Simchock - Keep your Goggles On, Center Strike the Hammer on the Chisel Hand, and Put 2-on-1-1-on-2. He's another throwback to a time when men being honorable was the norm. There was zero weakness on his crew. Pain, cold, bleeding, disfigured, rain, sick - it didn't matter. There was no complaining. Hardship nor toughness were glorified, focused on, talked about, or acknowledged in any way - EVER. It was just expected. Get the job done. Pull your weight. When it was too cold to lay mortared stone, Simchock would make up work for us to do, so we could still make some money. We'd make birdbaths, carve benches, or harvest stone out of the frozen ground (that ain't easy). It's citizens and business owners like him that are the backbone of America. He is an honorable man (and I need to take time to see him, the next time I'm out his way). Being around him made me a better person and taught me not to expect open praise for being what you were already supposed to be or doing what you were already supposed to be doing.

I'm fairly certain my Aunt **Marie** was spurring my Uncle **Doug** to enlist me from time-to-time, so I could help him with some of the projects he was working on (but I think I might have slowed him down, more than anything, though). My first time harvesting railroad ties and scything brush was with my Uncle Doug. I enjoyed putting my tough, callused Masculine Hands to the test, and I was very proud of our work. Later, when I was in college, I once ran into a snag getting all of my books. During a visit home, I told my Grandma about it, but not with the intent, expectation, or desire that I wanted or needed any help; I was simply relaying that I had a problem for which I needed to figure out a solution. But, it didn't take long before the money I needed showed up. I didn't know it at the time, but the source was my Uncle Doug. Like him, I don't need an audience or accolades to do the Right thing.

I remember my Aunt **Snip** buying me a footlocker from Roses department store, as I was on my way to college. She said it wasn't much, and in truth, it was a cheaply made, flimsy thing. It had completely fell apart in just a few years. I had to toss the bottom, but I kept the lid which I used as a tray. When the lid fell apart, I kept the lock and part of the plastic attached to it. It was a cherished piece, and I still miss having it. It reminded me of my aunt and the day she bought it for me. That leftover piece of lock and plastic lid was one of my most prized possessions for 15 years, until it got lost, during my divorce. My Aunt Snip taught me that Cost and Value are 2 very different things.

My Aunt **Joyce** used to have this old record player. I didn't think it was anything special, at the time, but looking back, it was built like a tank. It worked well and had a cassette tape feature, as well as a radio. She used to let me use that thing in a way that it wasn't designed to be used. This was around the time when Michael Jackson's "Thriller" album came out. I used to cut and mix songs on it by playing a bit of a song, recording it on the cassette, stopping at a cut point, and recording the next piece, to make dub versions of records. "Billie Jean" was one of my favorite victims for this work. She never got mad, irritated, or stopped me in any way. This allowed me to grow artistically and intellectually and was the gateway for MANY creative things I did later in life (including writing this book). My Aunt Joyce taught me that giving someone the latitude to learn and acquire new skills is priceless.

My Aunts **Roz** and **Margaret** were like the audience a performer wanted to show off for and impress. The questions they would ask would let you know that that they were paying close attention to what you were saying and even closer attention to what you were doing. I remember, while I was in college, that my Aunt Roz had sent me some money, about $50.00, so I could buy a bus ticket to go visit her. I was planning it and in a moment of weakness, I did the wrong thing and bought a bunch of food with it. In hindsight, I would have gotten way more food on a visit, but my primitive brain was blind to reason and logic. I apologized but she never accosted me for my Sell Out maneuver. It was like she didn't care and was happy that I got something of value, on her subsidy. This still bothers me, and to this day, if I give someone money for something, I remain empathetic, because that's what Aunt Roz would have done.

I used to have my most interesting, thought-provoking, weird, entertaining, and intellectually obtuse conversations with my Aunt **Debbie**. She used to plasticize my mind and was somewhat ahead of her time, regarding theoretical thought. I remember her talking about multiple dimensions, hidden government and world power structures, and the psyche's impact on physiology, in detail, long before other intellectuals I knew even began broaching the basics of those subjects. She may not have known the technical terminology for all of it, but she was a cerebral Beast, to me. Inspired by my interactions with her, I remember my writing becoming much more intense and unique. Some of my professors would ask me where I was getting the inspiration for that stuff, and I always said Heavy Metal Magazine, Marvel Comics, and my Aunt Debbie.

My Aunt **Brenda** was always teaching me something without me even knowing she did it. I only figured out years later that me acting Right half of the time was her doing. I thought it was me. Out of everything she did for me, there is one thing that stands out above everything else. While I was visiting with her, which I often did, she asked if I wanted dessert, since we had eaten real food a bit earlier. Of course I said I did. She asked me what I wanted, and I said rice. Now this dessert rice she used to make had milk, sugar, cinnamon, and probably a few more things in it. But one of the keys for her was the butter. She commented on how she liked to use so much that it was "yallah". That rice ranked right up there with the Chef Boy-Ar-Dee (with the hyphens) spaghetti my Aunt Debbie made me that had her own meatballs added, with the perfect amount of black pepper and salt. They made that stuff, just for me, and the currency of those memories are seared into my brain.

Mr. Philips was my Art teacher. He was the best teacher I ever had, in any subject, at any school. His class was a petri dish of expanded, unrestricted thought. Because latitude was boundless, thought exploration resulted in definitive conclusions on a thing. You could still be wrong, of course, but you now knew conclusively why you thought a certain way. In that class, I learned that most of the time, I didn't know what I actually thought about a thing, until I reasoned it out loud or wrote it down. He had worked to get me a full scholarship to one of the Art Institutes, but I was unable to attend. That was one of the biggest mistakes I ever made. Looking back, I would do whatever I needed to do, to leverage that scholarship.

Bob is a master mechanic, and for all intents and purposes, was the primary wrench turner on my 1970 Chevelle rebuild. I learned to re-build a car from the back to the front and from the ground up, from my step father Arch, so that is how I controlled the build. But, Bob is the one that got us past all of the inevitable difficulties that arise when doing this kind of figure-it-out-as-you-go work. When we go to car shows, Bob gets worked up, and I have to talk him back from the ledge of turning the Chevelle into a 9-second car, because he wants to "tub it and slap a roll cage in it". He can do it too. Having the right people around you who are assets adds tangible value to your life.

Arch always had the "I can figure it out" approach, to whatever he was working on. It didn't really matter what the challenge was, but he'd face anything directly. Although he's a conversationalist, there wasn't a whole lot of talk (and sometimes not a whole lot of planning), when there was work to be done; he took action. It wasn't impulsiveness as much as it was not delaying in dealing with something that was unavoidable. You know how in the movies there is a group of warriors standing outside of the monster's cave, with only one of them brave enough to go in? Arch is the one who would step into that cave. He would take on new challenges and try new things, giving 100% effort, even while sometimes having 100% lack of confidence. But he'd try anyway. He was more successful than not. I've suffered that same 100% lack of confidence, and I've adopted those same characteristics to overcome; he gave me the blueprint. As my stepfather, he always made me feel like he was proud to call me his son. He taught me that relatives and family aren't the same thing. His lessons have enabled me to embody that same approach of sincere allegiance and full commitment to folks who you may not share DNA with.

My cousin **Kenny** was my high school blueprint. He taught me to shake hands, web-to-web, with a firm grip, and solid eye contact. He also taught me to respect other men, and demand respect from them.

He said to not say you believed something you didn't, were into something you weren't, or approved of something you disagreed with, just because somebody else wanted you to. I don't think he ever knew how closely I watched him, but whenever I got into certain sticky situations, I'd ask myself, "What would Kenny do?". The stern admonition to "Be Your Own Man" would ring out in my head. From Kenny I learned to present myself as exactly what I am, plainly broadcast, with nothing hidden, and without apologizing.

My goal with my kids, **Kevin, X, and Jake**, was to teach them everything I could to toughen them and prepare them for the cruelties of the world. I told them to just follow The HodgeHouse Program until they were 18 and had graduated from high school, and on that day, they were fully their own men. True to my word, when the day came, I flipped a mental switch on our interactions and immediately became an optional advisor for them, if they wanted. I no longer commanded but instead would suggest things to think about or consider, but their choices were their own. They've all gone off to do various things with various levels of success. Some I talk to quite often, and some I talk to not at all. I still wouldn't change a thing, as the job I did to prepare them for the world was not done for me; it was done for them. Well, maybe I would change one thing. I would try to prepare them even better and let them spend more time with me camping off the grid, making fire using only sticks, creating long-term budgets, mastering understanding compound interest, and resolving real world problems.

I remember the 3-minute walk to visit my Aunt **Nancy**, when she lived in the apartments (converted from the historic Jubilee Hospital) down the street from me. I remember how I always felt more important when I left her, than I did when I arrived – that's priceless to me, even now. Whenever I was around her, even at my youngest, it "seemed" to me like she was slightly out of place. She had this regal air about her, and it was like she didn't exactly fit, in the small town we lived in. Her ideas were too big, and her presence needed space. You know how when you're at a venue, and somebody walks into the room, and half the people there stop what they're doing to glance in that person's direction? That's an "Aunt Nancy" they're looking at – powerful energy that projects out. As I got older and saw more of the world, I thought she would have been right at home on Fifth Avenue in New York City. My Aunt Nancy taught me to not dim the luster of my power, just so somebody else could feel better about how faint theirs was.

My **Mother** was a maverick. She struck out on her own after high school and was very successful. I remember her creating systems for everything. She'd stock up the hall closet with extra toothbrushes, toothpaste, soap, etc. She did the same thing with pantry and food items. Everything would be very organized. She would decide on a certain amount of a thing and keep that amount, backfilling as things were consumed. It seems simple and probably like no big deal. But, she was precise on how much of everything needed to be in stock – no more, no less. She never ran out of anything, because for anything taken a replacement was always put at the back of the line. This allowed flexibility in handling surprises, and she always knew what her capacity was for providing resources. She also had this budgeting system of putting money in specific, labeled envelopes. Once money was put in a particular envelope, it could only be used for whatever the label on the envelope indicated. I'm pretty sure, between her and PaPa, the seed was created that helped me develop my own systems. Almost everything I do today is done by first developing a framework or system and then executing.

Every boy wants their father to be their hero. My **Father** was that to me. He still is. One of my favorite shows, when I was growing up was "Magnum PI". He was like Magnum to me. He had the red car (OK, it was more like burgundy, but close enough), he had muscles, he had the mustache, and chicks dug him. Plus, he had the absolute coolest nickname on planet earth – "Devil Hodge". He was always adamant about being self-sufficient, taking care of yourself, and not depending on other people for things you could go out and hustle for, for yourself. He believed everyone should own their own business, even if they had another, regular corporate job. He also stressed always trying to improve some aspect of your life. I remember him fighting to get high school, graduating athletes into college. He was not only doing this alone, he was doing it while being undermined by the very people who SHOULD have actually been the ones trying to get them into college. I got to see it first hand. He believed that everybody should always be trying to level up and improve. Even now, he is still researching, studying, learning new things, and making plans on how to achieve his goals. Amazingly, even for things we have not previously discussed, our approaches to them are remarkably similar, even down to the details. He has been a singular, powerful motivating force, for me.

My **PaPa** taught me to love my calluses. It's like my callouses are old friends. I was about 9-years-old, when under his tutelage, I got my first ones – blisters that turned into rough, desensitized patches, that turned into thick, jagged, leathery armor. We used to sell starter plants – collard plants, tomato plants, and a few other things. I think it may have been something like 100 seedlings for $1.00 – not much money (but again, it trumpeted the "Work for Yourself" theme). The field was dug up with a shovel and the rows were made with a rake and hoe. That's it. I got so good using a shovel and other tools that he started hiring me out for jobs that otherwise would have taken heavy machinery. I remember one Christmas, he said he had an extra gift for me. He was visibly excited about it too. We went out to the toolshed and in the corner, on the left as you enter, was a brand new, long handled, flat head shovel. It had a bow on it and everything. And, man was I glad to get it – one of my top gifts of all time. I had worn the other flat head out. It was all flimsy feeling and distorted. But that new one was rock solid. My first year in college, I didn't do any physical labor. But, the carryover affect of those callouses was so strong that 12 months of soft living had minimal effect. I still had hands that would make others wince when shaking them, because the calluses on them were so jagged. I loved that. PaPa used to always say that the "Smallest Done Deed Beats the Biggest Best Intentions". Again, take action. I live by that.

My **Grandma** is an enigma. She's all mean and tough and sweet and kind, at the same time. And she can cook something delicious from almost nothing. EA still talks about the apple pie she made when he gave me a lift home, once. She will help anybody. ANYBODY. Now, she'll fuss at them for doing whatever stupid thing they did to "get into that mess" in the first place, but she will sacrifice everything to get them out of it. She didn't go much past elementary school but she is one of the most intelligent people I've ever been around. For years, I channeled her teachings when I was building teams of professionals, for work. Her lessons are front and center on nearly everything I do involving management. Even when I was a young kid, I knew she would get me ANYTHING I wanted. I came to the realization, when I was around 6, that I had to be careful and not ask for too much, because it was wrong to get everything you wanted, just because you could. I'm sure I was still spoiled, though. I pretty much limited my askings to comic books, activity books, novels, and cheeseburgers. Yup, she always made sure I read a lot and had plenty to eat. One of the things I took from her that I do to this day is to disconnect from the world early. I rarely take unexpected phone calls or visitors, after a certain time. My cutoff is 9pm but her's is 7pm. She facetiously asserts that nothing good happens, after that time, and if somebody's sick, call a doctor; if somebody's in trouble, call the law; if somebody's dead, call the morgue; but don't call me, until the morning. This is collectively one of the best lessons I've learned, on valuing and protecting my time and castle perimeter.

HodgeToo is my sweetie. She is all rainbows, sunshine, and happy feelings, and I'm all storm clouds, dark skies, and controlled aggression. It's the mating of a peppy, high speed sports car, full of fuel, with a grossly oversized, heavy restrictor plate. I am comfortable taking a chance on myself when it's just me, but she has made me comfortable taking a chance when it's us. I'd go so far as to say that she goes a step beyond support and exists more at the egging on stage, at this point. She has championed every single off-the-wall, weird, unorthodox plan I've had. I was unemployed and homeless, with atrocious credit and an unpredictable violent streak, at the start of us getting together. Yup, she sure can pick 'em. Not one time has she ever questioned my motives, plans, or dedication to improving our situation, or my ability to get things done. Heck, even the core manuscript for this book was written with her sitting 6 feet away from me, squoze into her Big Joe, in the Chillroom – pumping me up to "knock it out the box, Hodge", the entire time. One thing that most men experience that they may not talk about is the visceral pressure to perform and provide for their families. It makes it easier to dig Tunnels in Turds when the folks you are doing it for let you know they appreciate your efforts for them and do not disdain you, just because you smell bad doing it.

These moments and these people (as well as a few others) have helped to create me and make me what I am, whether that be good or bad. All of these little yesterdays that I have socked away are the anchors I use that keep me grounded and thankful, because I don't deserve what I have. I literally think about these people and these things every day. This kaleidoscopic menagerie of human riches gives me clarity of purpose. Although my passion with it all runs deep and strong, my cognitive malformation is that I deliberately attenuate all emotions and feelings, shunning comforts and wants, when an objective is defined – and vexingly, I am always working towards some objective. I prefer to take the Long Way on the Hard Road, for most things. The only thing that matters, once I'm ON, is the Work. I purposefully harden my heart to my tasking, and Take Action. Any of the salty water I might have, from the vulnerability of slumber, is left on the pillow, and my head is never resting on that for long.

Hodgerian Crom-Hammer

You have Breath in your Lungs and Will in your Heart, so Understand that in Truth, **you Want for NOTHING**. With these, All Else can be Attained. The Excellence of your Execution, the Honor of Your Actions, and the Results of your Decisions mean Everything.

Your Excuses mean Nothing.

— Charles Hodge
(Hodge, 2016)

INTRODUCTION

DON'T TRUST ME

This book is a mixture of my opinions, guesses, and even a few of what could arguably be called, empirical if not outright, established facts. But, what makes something a fact? Is it based on science? Science is often updated, and earlier assertions, laws, principles, etc. are proven wrong. Is it based on religion? There are a lot of those, with many having undeniably immaculate principles, but they also possess myriad contradictions, as well as antithetical notions between them. Is it based on the sheer number of people, institutions, and learned bodies that assert a notion that causes a thing to be factual? The **mobile vulgus** is notoriously inaccurate, when it comes to being on the Right side of most issues. So, I can't even answer what I think makes something an actual Fact, and I won't struggle to do so, now. But, opinions, we can all have those, even with no articulable or justifiable reason, for having one. Even so, I personally like having a reason, even for my opinions, and I attempt to back them up with data, if not (what we loosely might call) Facts. And, if I channel ESPN Analyst Ryan Clark's sentiment on the matter, I can have any opinion I want; **I don't have to be Right – I just need to have a good reason for being Wrong**.

Each and every one of us is responsible for our own decisions and our actions related to those decisions. We can draw inspiration, guidance, knowledge, and suggestions from others, but our choices are our own. Of course, this is much less so, for those who are younger or immature. However, the older we get and the more experience we gather, the less justification we have to project our responsibilities of choice on others. If you are in your late teens or early 20s, and you are still asserting that someone outside of yourself is responsible for any of your poor decisions, stop being a victim and take ownership of your life. This book presents information, much of which is actionable. However, every person's situation, motivations, goals, resources, challenges, etc. are different. It is up to you to decide which elements of this book may be relevant to you, and then use what I have presented as a catalyst to do more research and explore more facets, before taking meaningful action. Independent research is the default first action I recommend every person take. Regardless of how emphatic, aggressive, or matter-of-fact a suggested course of action is presented, from any source, **YOUR DECISIONS ARE YOUR OWN**.

CONVENTIONS

This entire work is somewhat of a stream of consciousness mishmash of random thoughts that I've attempted to glue together in something resembling a book. Because sometimes it's difficult to fully relay what you're thinking with the written word, I've included a lot of illustrations. The illustration bloat serves to, hopefully, keep reader interest and simplify understanding. I was going for that stuffy, not-too-self-righteous, college textbook, mixed and diluted with a just-the-facts-but-goofy, elementary school workbook type of vibe – an unholy, mongrelized, literary offspring, for sure.

I use a variety of fonts, font sizes, line spacings, etc., similar to what a magazine would use. I needed to do this to give me enough control and latitude over the layout, so everything would fit, when space got tight. I tried to emphasize information density without compromising readability. Punctuation does not follow the Chicago Manual of Style, as I have punctuated it the way I want. This is particularly noticeable with quotes, as I place all quotes before any terminating punctuation, like "this". I also Capitalize, ALL CAPS, and **bold** certain words for emphasis, whether they follow convention or not. I also did not follow strict APA for the Index, but I stayed consistent on how I did it.

I'll sometimes purposefully misuse singular and plural words. Most frequently, I'll treat the word "data" as if it's its singular form, "datum" (did you catch the double "its"?). I do this, because although I'm using the word "data", in my mind I'm thinking "dataset".

And, there are some terms in here that are not actually words, or at least words you can find in the dictionary, because I made them up (except for "irregardless"). I use them, because I think they convey what I was attempting to say the best. You'll have to ferret out their meanings, based on the usage and context. Some, but not all, examples include:

- **ennourish -** I think it adds nuance to plain old "nourish".
- **dubiousized -** It sounds like something Don King would say, so I had to roll with it.
- **theorectal/theorectical -** A false belief or assumption that causes a Cranial-Rectal Inversion that screws you over.
- **fraudery -** Come on, man! This should already be a word.
- **irregardless -** I don't care that it's not considered a standard word, I like using it. Besides, I believe it may have come into common usage, due to a linguistic mutation over time, perhaps originating from something like **"aye regardless"** or **"ere regardless"**.

A WORD ON A.I.

I have not used any direct A.I. resources, to my knowledge, for this work. I know that there is a proliferation of created content that is the result of prompt engineering. I am not using that. Eventually, I may acquire a taste for using it, find that it makes sense to use it, or discover that its use is largely unavoidable. But, for now, I disdain its general use and abhor its heavy use. I want to avoid it, as much as I can, for as long as I can, especially for things that I can do myself. Eventually, we will all suffer, due to skill erosion and retarded development, if we individually fail to exercise the gifts in our intellectual and artistic tool chests.

Many images are taken from my online resource library, so some of those could have used A.I. elements, but I have no way of knowing, for certain. For the actual writing, aside from direct sources that have been noted, it is all taken from my musings - every single word. I essentially sat down with a blank page and began transcribing my thoughts. Additionally, nearly all of my research actually took place AFTER I had completed the initial manuscript text, mainly because I thought some of my assertions needed to have some kind of source identified. My simply saying with certainty something assumed or stated was so (unintended consonance bomb), just because I wrote it down, was not sufficient. This does raise the question about how much A.I. saturation is or is not involved with a simple word search, or query for concept clarification, or online tool request. And, I have also noticed several vendors repackaging previously existing tools and capabilities as A.I., even though nothing has fundamentally changed with their offerings. So, which products are using A.I. proper, rather than solely leveraging the marketing prowess the semantics of the term provides? I am not sure.

Sometimes, during **VER/VAL** (Verification and Validation), I ended up discovering that my notions and assertions were completely wrong, and I very much enjoyed unmasking the correct information. Although I possess physical copies for most of my sourced information, I notated using internet sources, if possible, to make it easier for people to go to a link, and verify the information for themselves (even if I have the actual, physical book). Personally, I enjoy reading a real, physical copy of a book, for most things. I like the feel of the pages, the whisper a sheet coos at you when you turn it, the slight kiss of breeze the paper exhales as it snuggles in to spoon with its peers, and the different scents and aromas that waft up from the leaves, the covers, and the bindings. Electronic media has its place, for sure, especially when searching for a specific term or concept, but to me, there is nothing, absolutely nothing, like flipping through a real, physical book.

FISICALITY

SECTION 1

PREFLIGHT

Foundation and Philosophy

THE POWER OF TIME

Time is your most precious resource. It is perishable, limited, irretrievable, irreplaceable, and unstoppable. As far as my cautious understanding of it goes, the threads of Time, along with it's cosmic peer, Space, form the fabric of our reality. Amazingly, for such an important element of the human condition, we don't respect Time very much. We waste it, disregard it, and throw it away – that is, until it has nearly ran out. Then, all of a sudden, Time is all we can think about. Remember that research paper you were assigned 2 months ago that you couldn't seem to fit into your schedule to start working on? Well, it's due in 3 days now, and you find yourself, somehow, unbelievably energized and focused to get it done. Sleep – who needs it? Food – that's for lesser beings. Urination – hold it until your body reabsorbs it. Shower – simply wallow in your own filth. You don't have TIME for those things.

Well, one of the things my PaPa told me was, "Time isn't something you **have**, it's something you **take**". There is so much wisdom in that simple statement, for me, including the notion of a person having some control over Time's impact on them. Now, you can't control Time itself, but you can control some of its impacts on you. It all comes down to choice. You can sensibly CHOOSE to take the Time to work on that next paper a little each week, and reap the benefits of reduced stress, which can potentially lead to improved health and a more balanced lifestyle. And, Oh yeah, you will probably also write a better paper.

Oftentimes, we must pull back and change our perspective or distance from a thing, to fully grasp or appreciate Time's impact on it. An ice cube left out on the high-noon, sun-warmed asphalt, during the hottest days of the summer, in Florida, shows the effects of Time very quickly to us - in minutes - seconds, even. However, the degradation of that same asphalt under that same type of sun takes place much slower than that of the ice cube - in months - years, even. Similarly, the results-based changes, from the choices we make in our lives, can be even slower still - years - decades, even. I've heard a remix of Edwin Stanton's assertion, that a man of 50 chooses his face, that says, **"When you are born, you look like your parents, but when you die, you look like your decisions"** (Chittenden, 1891).

With all of that said, I'm not sure I can think of a more impactful, controllable, and conspicuous representation of a person's life decisions made manifest, along with Time's impact on them, than that of how they have chosen to leverage our current money system. I advocate investing in a security, reinvesting the dividends (if it pays one), and simply never withdrawing any of the money, as it grows via appreciation and compounding. It's the simplest thing in the world to do. The hardest part of that whole scenario is trying to decide which security to buy. Personally, I'm a value investor, which means I want to buy a well-ran company, with solid financial fundamentals, at a discount. But, even by simply using the standard benchmark of the S&P 500, the maxim about the value of Time in the Market beating Timing the Market can be easily proven. For example, using "The S&P 500 Periodic Investment Calculator" found at https://dqydj.com/sp-500-periodic-reinvestment-calculator-dividends/, a $1,000 initial investment with an additional $100 monthly recurring investment in the S&P 500 for 30 years, beginning in July of 1994 and ending in July of 2024, results in a total of $37,000 invested and a final value of $213,813. However, for those who were able to invest an initial $12,000 with **no recurring** monthly contributions for the same time period, the final value is $220,696. This is a modestly higher return but with $25,000 less invested – same stock, much less invested, less interaction, and a larger final value. And, if for some reason a diversified portfolio that has a few multibaggers in it is used, the returns could be even higher.

HOW TO START

You don't need a money manager, financial advisor, financial planner, or wealth manager. You might need a coach, or an instructor, and definitely a CPA (a good CPA is invaluable), but anybody who says they need to take administrative control of your finances is not needed. You have what it takes to begin learning the skills needed to successfully control your finances. Besides, you would be hard pressed to find someone who cares more about the outcomes of your financial decisions than you do. When starting out as a self-taught anything, you exist simultaneously as the parent and the child; you are your own intellectual progenitor. As the parent, you want to be a good parent to your Money Management Child Self. Good parents modify their ecosystem and create rigid, protective structures for their offspring. This keeps the offspring safe from outside threats, as well as from self-harm. For your Money Management Journey, this means you must choose proven educational resources, optimize your learning environment, and create an intelligent execution plan.

As the days turn into weeks, that turn into months, that turn into years,

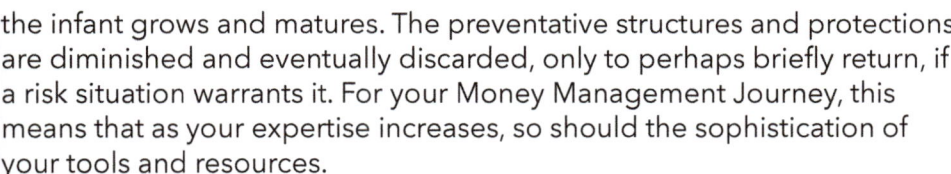

the infant grows and matures. The preventative structures and protections are diminished and eventually discarded, only to perhaps briefly return, if a risk situation warrants it. For your Money Management Journey, this means that as your expertise increases, so should the sophistication of your tools and resources.

Bad parents tend to not provide many meaningful restrictions and allow disrespect, tantrums, and entitled behavior to flourish, early in the child's developmental cycle. Eventually, as the child is transitioning into adulthood or has fully transitioned into adulthood, the parent finally begins inserting themselves into the child's life, in a feeble, unwelcomed attempt to try to parent like they should have done 2 decades earlier. For your Money Management Journey, this means you need to focus on perfecting the basics from the very beginning, rather than waiting to learn them later on, when you are in harm's way, out of time, and unprepared.

The best parents, however, go so far as to expose their children to risks and challenges on purpose, albeit in controlled situations and/or with monitoring, to foster the child's physical and intellectual development, resilience, toughness, and capability. The job of a good parent is to protect their offspring, **when they need it but not when they don't**, pass along knowledge, if they themselves have it, deliver wisdom, if they themselves possess it, and prepare their offspring for life's many unavoidable hardships. For your Money Management Journey, this means that as you become comfortable with using larger sums of money that you also place restrictions and limits on the amounts used, especially when using new techniques.

Ultimately, from a Hodgerian perspective, the best parents take away as much as reasonably possible that is external to the child, while still completely nourishing their intellectual, mental, emotional, and spiritual coffers. They don't parent by giving them **THINGS**. Bad parents do the exact opposite of all of that. They parent by giving them **THINGS** but fail to nourish them intellectually, mentally, spiritually, or emotionally. They add unneeded protections and gifts, without context, hampering development, independence, and knowledge of the Self. For your Money Management Journey, this means that you must not rely on fads, tricks, unnecessary tooling, and additional cash injections for success. You can't outspend bad planning and poor preparation. The best parents give their kids that which you cannot see but that which can readily be seen. Here, you must choose to do the things that will make you a good parent to your evolving Child Self (remember, you are your own advocate and your own intellectual progenitor).

Be aware that, as you grow and improve, **forces will align against**

you; it is inevitable. Your friends and relatives will undermine you. It may be a parent, roommate, co-worker, spouse, or sibling that is actively hampering, or even outright sabotaging your efforts. The source of challenges is not limited to people you personally know but also companies, organizations, institutions, and community groups. So, not only will entities and people stand in your way, they will actively plot against you, seeking to stifle your progress at every turn. ChexSystems, LexisNexis, Equifax, Experian, TransUnion, the banks, etc. have created labyrinthine, information complexes, seemingly to frustrate and discourage you from retrieving your own personal information. You'll find that web forms don't work, CAPTCHA has infinite loops, web portals crash mysteriously, unknown errors and technical difficulties force you to use their snail mail options, etc. Don't be discouraged by these phenomena, and don't dwell on the absurdity. It is enough to know that they exist, to be prepared for them when they happen, and to keep moving forward, starving them of your energy, at all costs. You can choose to empower the thing that will make you successful or the thing that will destroy you. Or, as told in the Cherokee parable, the choice is yours, but know that **which ever Beast you feed is the one that will become stronger**, eventually consuming the other Beast and you. Feed the Right Beast. Your life depends on it.

OBJECTIVE

The main objective of this book is to show you how to get to the point where the bulk of your earnings is directed towards buying assets and to assist with you gaining mastery over your financial life, rather than being a slave to it; slaves, by definition, own nothing. Don't be a slave. Become an owner of something. The very act of owning something, striving for something, or acquiring something forces your brain to think differently. It is a catalyst for growth. The asset can be tangible, as in a rare painting or precious jewels, or intangible, as in an acquired skill or honed ability. Acquiring assets siphons energy and thought away from time wasters and comforting liabilities and redirects that energy and thought to your beneficial and enriching assets. People who strive for nothing have little reason to attempt any kind of growth, aside from that engendered by **Bread & Circuses**.

Some characteristics of people who are owners with assets are that they are good citizens, they are thoughtful during interactions, they contribute to society in positive ways, they are empathetic, they are giving, and their thought process revolves around long-term thinking. These are just some of the characteristics, but let me justify my assertions. They are thoughtful, because they are responsible for more than just themselves. They are empathetic, because they must be aware of how others view the things they own, so that those things frictionlessly fit into their communities. They contribute to society in positive ways, because they fundamentally recognize their individual impact in and on their communities. They are more giving, because they know that elevating those around them ensures that what they have is better protected, due to their immediate community not suffering from lack or want. Their thought process is long-term because they have to account for and make determinations about the impact of their actions or inactions. Notice, none of those reasons were necessarily **benevolent** or out of the good of one's heart, as much of what makes someone a good owner is **pragmatic** thought. However, if there are additional reasons that are benevolent, there is an argument to be made that we are all better off for it, but it is not a necessity.

Whether rich, poor, wealthy, or broke, people who own nothing or who are responsible for nothing are limited in their options for delivering Value to the rest of society, their country, their community, their neighborhood, or even their immediate household. They are less likely to clean up after themselves, they are less likely to groom themselves, they are usually entitled, they usually demand from others things they can't even provide for themselves or things they are unwilling to give to others, they don't vote, and they are typically a burden to those around them. Most of what they have to offer are intangibles and talk, which can potentially be beneficial but are often just tripe and drivel. Even the small child who earned his first bike through chores thinks differently than the child who received his first bike, just because he gets everything he asks for. So, yes, become an asset owner. Asset acquisition, especially earned asset acquisition, is a proven path to fiscal freedom, so I encourage you to make it a primary objective in your life. It can readily be done in tandem with every other thing you have going on. You can easily scale the effort up or down, based on your available bandwidth and resources, but no matter what, ensure that you endeavor to consistently acquire assets.

Here, we will loosely define an asset as something that benefits you, in some way, more than it detracts from you, by which ever metric(s) you decide to use. For example, your home can be thought of as an asset, in that, you live in it, you might get some kind of social at-a-boys for living in a nice one, you can keep your stuff in it, it provides you with protection, and you can sell it to make money. However, depending on your circumstances, any mortgage attached to your house is not an asset; it detracts from your fiscal stability, investment capability, and quality of your life, in every way. And, even without a mortgage, you still have taxes, maintenance, repairs, etc. to deal with. **A House is built from the outside in; a Home is built from the inside out.**

So, based on the way I've written this, your HOME is an asset, but your HOUSE is not, even though they both map back to the same entity. And a house only becomes a home, once the impact of it's liabilities are subordinate to its benefits (think of the song popularized by Luther Vandross, here). This is the sweet spot. People don't say, "House Sweet House". They say, "Home Sweet Home". Even if we can now classify a Home as an asset, **we may not be able to classify it as a serviceable asset**, because if you need it to live in, you can't leverage it by selling it. You may be able to rent a room or extract some equity via a loan, but as far as getting $500,000 of asset value out of a $500,000 Home, your only recourse is to sell it. This results in you needing to find somewhere else to stay which could consume all of your profit, negating the benefit. So, is a legitimate asset still an asset, if you can't leverage it? Well, it is, but it needs to be given some kind of **Reality Weighting**. This means that even for a legitimate asset, you will be well served in calculating what you think its actual Usable Asset Value is, rather than just its projected Asset Market Value.

ANTIPODEAN ENTITIES

Arguably, one of the most impactful classes of assets and liabilities is the Antipodean Entity. This is an element in your life that has the ability to quickly switch between being an asset or a liability, at a moment's notice, sometimes multiple times a day. These are the things that can fool you and give you confidence in a false reality, that's tethered to an induced expectation of something that does not actually exist. Michael McDonald said it best with the Doobie Brothers:

**What a Fool Believes He Sees,
No Wise Man has the Power to Reason Away.**

- The Doobie Brothers
(McDonald & Loggins, 1978)

Things in this class include items such as your lawn landscaping (it adds curb appeal, enjoyment of the household, and protection – but it also takes time, money, and effort to maintain); your internet connection (it connects you to the outside world, acts as a resource with nearly unlimited access to knowledge, and offers access to resource portals that simplify time-consuming tasks – but it can also be a gateway to criminal activity, time decay via gaming, and self-abuse addiction via adult content); and your gym membership (it can help you maintain a healthy lifestyle, serve as a venue for positive, social interaction, and provide access to cutting edge technology that helps you quickly reach personal

fitness goals – but it can also expose you to toxic people, destructive activities, relationship infidelity, as well as self-esteem degradation, if you don't go consistently; or it can be a financial drain, if you don't go at all). The Antipodean Entity is a **chameleon** that will eventually fall primarily into either the asset or liability category, based on its overall body of work within your lifestyle or your wielding of it. There are assets and there are liabilities, and each of those can appreciate or depreciate to the point that they switch identities. For example, that old, raggedy, piece of junk Chevy that is taking up needed space in the barn is a liability – UNTIL it gets appraised at over $250,000 for being an all original, 1970 Chevelle 454 LS6 and becomes an asset. And, that rental property was a cash flow monster and asset a decade earlier – UNTIL it became an albatross around the owner's neck, after the paper mill moved in next door, fouled the air for 2 square miles, tanked property values, and drove renters away. The takeaway here is to remain vigilant and not take as rote, the qualities of anything, in the midst of ever-changing conditions.

But, the most impactful Antipodean Entity is the collective of people you have around you. A person is either an asset or a liability and can switch between being either of those within minutes or even seconds, depending on the situation. Now, I'm not advocating that anybody does a purely clinical examination of their social circle and throw away meaningful relationships, but I am advocating that folks take an assessment of the people around them, and decide if those people enrich or detract from their contentment and quality of life. As an aside, from my perspective, although often overlooked and disregarded, **the elderly are some of the most Value Dense assets on the planet**.

Too often I see people heavily investing in failing, underperforming human assets (or even outright human liabilities), while simultaneously starving their high yield, high quality, high performing human assets of resources. The 6-time loser gets a Fresh-Out party thrown for them, a fat cash roll for pocket change, and the spare room to crash in, until he can "get back on his feet". The guy that's paying the lion's share of the bills for everybody else in the house can't have the dinner leftovers for his next day's lunch, can't get his side hustle flyer put up with the others on the bulletin board, and can't borrow an unused car to get to a job interview. Personally, I refuse to channel my resources into known, habitually underperforming assets or liabilities, in any meaningful way. For those of you who are merciful (or gullible), I encourage you to at least distribute your resources, and also,

Invest in the people who have Potential, not just the ones who have Problems.

ASSET ACQUISITION LIFE CYCLE

For those who are driven and goal oriented, it is important to choose the human assets that best align with you and not be impaired by overexposing yourself to people whose goals, desires, ethics, morality, trustworthiness, loyalty, industriousness, or willingness to commit don't align with yours. For any asset, of any kind, its Asset Acquisition Life Cycle really only has 3 steps:

Asset Acquisition Life Cycle

1. **Acquire a specific asset (stock, property, friend, etc.).**
2. **Reinvest any benefits (dividends, equity, camaraderie, etc.).**
3. **Hold the asset forever, unless it no longer aligns with your investment thesis, becomes a detriment, or becomes untrustworthy (sell, donate, discard, cut ties, etc.).**

From an investment perspective, these 3 simple steps are really the essence of how to exploit the time value of money. Here, it is important to distinguish between **saving** money and **investing** money. Even though many people lump those two things together, saving and investing actually have very little to do with each other, just like saving 20 apples has very little to do with planting 20 apple seeds. And, for the following analogy, the exact same things happen to the apples that you save and the money that you save. Here, we posit that 1 apple equals $100, for the example. The 20 saved apples can certainly sustain you for a short while, maybe even several weeks. But over time, they start to dry out, lose their sheen, become susceptible to pests, decay, and eventually become worthless, except perhaps as fertilizer. Similarly, the saved $2,000 can sustain you for a short while, maybe even several weeks. But, over time, it starts to diminish in value, experiences inflation-reduced buying power, becomes susceptible to undisciplined withdrawals, and eventually becomes worthless, except perhaps as meager pocket change.

The planted seeds and invested money, however, experience a completely different life cycle. The planted seeds are initially unable to sustain you. In fact, they are burdensome, as they require resources (soil, light, water, and tending). Some will never sprout, some will sprout but die, some will struggle to flourish, perhaps for years, and a fortunate few will quickly flourish, from the very start. But eventually, for the younglings that survive, their growth becomes exponential, they become self sustaining with minimal tending required, and most importantly, they start to bear fruit. You now have magnitudes more than the original 20 apples you started with. You now have more than enough to sustain yourself, sell some, give some away, and use some to plant even more trees, increasing your bounty.

Similar to the planted apple seeds, the invested $2,000 is initially unable to sustain you. In fact it is burdensome, as it will require resources (research, discipline, additional influxes of cash, and management). Some investments will fail immediately, some will initially increase in value, before irreversibly falling in value. Some will trend up but mostly sideways, perhaps for years, and some will generate healthy returns from the very start. But eventually, for the securities that survive, their growth becomes exponential, they become fiscally accretive, via capital appreciation, and most importantly, they start paying a dividend. **Your asset is now making you money from nothing**. And, I mean it's using absolutely NOTHING, no other mechanism, aside from your owning it. You don't have to manage it, approve sick days, deal with scandal-induced media fallout, restructure debt, deal with vendors, or even check to see if it clocked in. You could literally sleep late every day, watch cartoons, workout whenever you wanted, hangout with your pals, or play video games, and still make money. **You will make this money every day, 24 hours a day, every week, every month, every year, year in and year out.** And, usually, the only thing that will mess a system like this up, once it's established, is a Black Swan Event or you monkeying around with the principle. Don't touch it. Leave it alone. The principle is off limits. The principle feeds the machine; it is the power source. The dividends become your new salary, and they are deployed as such. Treat them like a paycheck. This means that a portion of the dividend payout is used for your schemes and plans, whether that be living expenses, luxuries, or incidentals – but only a portion. The rest goes back towards feeding the machine, i.e. increasing the principle. As a final thought on this section, the stress you experience from saving money continues to increase, the longer that that money is saved; the stress you experience from investing money in solid assets continues to decrease, the longer that that money remains invested.

MONEY MANAGEMENT PATH

We are all one natural disaster, medical event, legal settlement, unwise decision, car crash, lottery win, or disloyal romantic episode away from a financial happenstance that could potentially wipe out all of our funds. So, it makes sense to create as much fiscal cushion as we can, while we can. If you're not investing in assets, saving money is exponentially better than wasting money, but if saving money without intent is the furthest you've gotten, it only shows that you know very little about the basics of wealth creation and Money Management. At best, you may be a passable money manager, but you are ignorant of wealth management. This is not an insult; it is an observation. For example, as of June 2024, the average APY for a savings account is 0.58%, while the rate of inflation is 3.36%. This means every dollar sitting in the average savings account is losing 2.78% of its value, every single year it stays there, using those rates. A pure savings account, along with some of its derivatives, do not preserve cash asset value. Enjoying cash, as an asset, only occurs if it is put to work in some way that delivers a positive return on the principle that outpaces inflation, while also preserving that same principle. From the moment money is deposited into a typical (rather than high yield) savings account, it is losing value, due to inflation. The only way to preserve or increase cash asset value is to deploy money into appreciating assets.

Money is fickle. It's like that hot chick that everybody wants to date and that people will do anything to get. If she's yours, your closest friends will try to steal her away. Strangers will lie and cheat to possess her. People will compromise their morals, break the law, and even kill, for her. In order to keep her, you've got to pay her some attention and be savvy in how you deal with her. **Money doesn't just sit still.** It is always moving. It is like water, ever seeking to flow to new places, the easy places to get to, slipping through cracks and away from you, unless you direct it to where you want it to go. You can only hold on to it by keeping it occupied, putting it to work, or deploying it. If you somehow contain it, in say a savings account, a jar in the closet, or box buried in the back yard, it will become stagnant and dry up. So the suggested course of action is to deploy cash to acquire appreciating assets. By their very nature, appreciating assets may also depreciate, so your choices must be wise. For pure cash deployment vehicles, stocks, bonds, ETFs, money market accounts, and certificates of deposit are all viable options, depending on your investment thesis.

From my perspective, the savings account use case is valuable but limited to being a temporary storage area for a pending purchase, or as a holding tank for earmarked funds that must maintain maximum liquidity and transferability. However, there are some account types that seem to straddle the line between savings and investing, such as a certificate of deposit account. Even though, a CD won't make you rich via its exponential growth, it will preserve what you have and should slightly outpace inflation, if you invest properly.

If I had to create the general levels for a realistic, **Basic Money Management Path**, they would look something like this:

1. **Waste All Of Your Money**
    This is where we all start. We have very little knowledge and may not have received much in the way of instruction from parents,

friends, or institutions. We primarily make and take action on theorectical decisions. Most to nearly all of our money goes towards things we don't need, impulse buys, gambling, treats, empty calories, substances, or other destructive endeavors.

2. **Enjoy Undisciplined Spending**

   We've learned a little bit at this stage and suffered through a few things, so this is where we still waste money but not as much, as before. We are now starting to divert some money more towards purchases for things that we actually need or that enrich us, but it is uncontrolled spending. For example, if we need a vehicle, at this stage, we tend to buy a new one with all the trimmings that is out of our sensible price range, rather than a well-maintained, used one.

   RED WAREHOUSE EXERCISE

   Here's an exercise I like to do from time to time. Select a time period of 6-12 months in the past. Take 10 minutes to write down a list of everything you can recall buying, during that time. If you use a credit card, that makes it easier, as it will provide an authoritative record. Feel free to group stuff like eating out, recurring bills, etc., however be sure to still capture one-offs, especially your larger purchases, as separate items. Now imagine that everything you bought was arranged in the middle of a large, red warehouse, laid out in rows that you could peruse. For each item, determine how much you use it and how valuable it has been to you. There is an attendant, attired in a crimson and ebony suit. For each item, he asks if you would rather keep the item you bought or be given your money back. Make this scenario real, in your mind. Imagine it to be true. Imagine having your money returned to you and anything associated with the unwanted purchase, wiped away, with no questions asked and no penalty. If you find that you have several items that you would rather erase from your purchase history than keep, it means you need to start making better buying decisions, slow down on executing purchases, and maybe even start doing without a few things.

3. **Start Saving Money Without Intent**

   Here, we've grown to the point where we know that it makes sense to not spend it, just because we have it, and to put aside some money, for later. We don't know what we are saving it for, and the savings have no purpose, but we're saving it anyway. This is infinitely better than what we were doing in the last step, and this is where most people end up. As folks are growing up, they are told that responsible people save money, so they do it in an attempt to do the Right thing. Unfortunately, most of us are not only **undereducated,** we are also **miseducated**, when it comes to money matters.

4. **Start Saving Money With Intent**

   This is where we turn the corner towards being an effective Money Manager. We have placed limits on undisciplined spending and are saving money with intent. We start labeling the money that we're saving, based on its purpose, and may even begin to create different accounts for categorized allocations. Here, the money for the new living room furniture, vacation cruise, and Benelli M4 remains distinct and segregated.

5. **Allocation to Retirement/Bonds/Certificates/Investing/Etc.**

   At this stage, we embrace full adulthood thinking. We adopt habits that provide fiscal stability and minimize risk, while also diversifying our financial assets and planning for the future. We become hyperfocused, and our confidence drastically increases.

6. **Aggressive Asset Ownership**

   We have probably reduced our Debt Load at this point, but on paper, we may also still have as much debt as we've had in the previous steps, due to circumstance (buying a house, for instance). However, as our fiscal management approach is different, our decisions are different. Even though the Debt Load is the same, the quality of what that debt was used for has increased. Instead of going into debt to get new spinners for the two unreliable cars we have that just aren't running quite right, we go into debt with some buddies to purchase a duplex that we Sweat Equity Renovate and rent out. Our focus has changed to that of asset acquisition and leverage exploitation. We are obsessed with it but not in a detrimental way. We use nearly every penny not pre-allocated to budgeted items as capital to grow our asset base, while also continuing to reduce debt.

7. **Explore More Sophisticated Fiscal Structures and Vehicles**

   This final stage is where we start exploring more advanced Money Management tools and techniques, such as options trading, Buy-Borrow-Die, becoming a franchisee, or exploring creating a Family Bank. The growth continues from here.

INFORMATION AGENTS

Determining who to listen to can be daunting, especially when it comes to money. For money advice, do you listen to your banker? Your homeroom teacher? Or, maybe you should listen to your football coach? What about your parents? Nah, your video game buddy has the answers? Or better yet, the Trust Fund Baby who hangs out around your favorite bar? Nope, it's probably better to tune into to one of those financial gurus on the nightly news channel or social media? Perhaps you should just get a bunch of books that are supposed to be good, according to a web search? My suggestion is to listen to all of the above and more but only for data gathering, because regardless of who you listen to, the decision of what you do with your money is yours and yours alone. However, there are some considerations. Personally, I tend to classify individuals into several categories, when it comes to information agents and their ideas. They are The Audience, The Amateur, The Thief, The Creator, and the Artist.

The Audience - May be able to either create something that is functional or deliver something that is functional, but they can't do both and sometimes can do neither.

The Amateur - Can create and/or deliver a highly capable product, and they are honest about their abilities and shortcomings. They acknowledge the superiority of True Creators and Artists.

The Thief - Can skillfully deliver content but can't create it. It's akin to someone speaking perfect Spanish, even though they can't actually converse using the language. They've only learned how to mimic the sounds, the inflection, and delivery. This still takes talent, but it is exposed as fraudery when challenged, questioned, or asked to explain anything Beyond the Mimic. Because he didn't create it, any response he gives in regards to the creation is either silence, a guess, or a lie. And the silence is much more damaging than the lie, because it delivers a visceral, prevaricated, false narrative that leads people astray, as they take credit for others' work, claim it as their own, and refuse to recognize the original work or creator (thanks, to Joe Rogan, for channeling Robert Louis Stevenson on the analogy).

The Creator - Creates all aspects of a thing and understands how everything works (inspiration, source, development, final version, implementation, and best delivery).

The Artist - Can create and deliver. This is the highest level. Prince is a perfect example for this category, from the musical realm, as he could write, produce, record, arrange, and perform, entire albums completely alone, and then execute a live performance, in front of a crowd, that outclassed the recorded version.

So, I reiterate, listen to everyone. But, give more veritable weight to those you place in the Creator and Artist categories, with the understanding that sometimes the Artist is the homeless guy camped outside of the gas station, and The Thief is the prestigious expert on TV who lives in the multi-million dollar mansion.

TRUE DESIRES

In order to be Truly successful, a person needs to be honest about what their True desires are. Often times, we tell people everything that they want to hear (or think they want to hear, because sometimes, those people aren't even being honest about the outcomes they actually want to see either). If you can't be honest with anyone, above all else, at least be honest with yourself about yourself. We SAY we value honesty, family, justice, clean living, relationships, excellence, etc. But we SHOW that we value lying, gossip, pettiness, intoxication, and infidelity. From what I've personally witnessed, **the more upstanding and honorable people seem in public, the more you had best pay close attention to what they say and do, to ferret out their degeneracy and deceit**.

To restate a sentiment attributed to James W. Frick, you don't have to tell ME what's important to you and what you Value; show me what you spend your time and money on, and I'll tell YOU what's important to you and what you Value. You say your kids are important to you; I say they are not, but your hanging out with the fellas 5 nights out of 7 is important to you. You say your wife is important to you; I say she is not, but that the women you sleep around with are important to you. You say Family is important to you; I say it is not but that gossip, undermining, and backbiting is important to you. You say having a well-ran household is important to you; I say it is not, but blowing money on fun, cars, trips, and knickknacks, while the house remains in disrepair is important to you. I could go on, but you get the point. Before undertaking any endeavor, first be honest with yourself and forthright about what you want and what you are willing to do to get it. Once you are fully aware and accepting of what you are really about, you can decide which parts of yourself you don't like and which parts you truly want to change. Then, and only then, can you begin to make meaningful changes that have some staying power.

MANHOOD AND RESPONSIBILITY

Understanding the ways of being able to proficiently manage one's finances is especially important for men and critically important for young men. From my perspective, poor men, without a plan, who don't have initiative, who waste resources without having resources, and are slothful, should not date, have a girlfriend, or seek any kind of romantic interaction. Any man with that mix of characteristics needs to retool and learn to focus on achievement; there is no time for romance, for them (in my humble opinion). I suggest these folks spend some quality, intimate time with themselves, to neutralize any erotic urges, and get back to work. You can be poor, and you can not have a plan, and you can not have initiative, but you can't be all three, at the same time. A man like that is good for something between NOT MUCH and NOTHING AT ALL. Although some of them may fool you for a while, you can easily spot them, as they will be the ones who don't even brush their teeth or bathe every day.

Additionally, these individuals who DO very little, often have a lot to say. They are experts at everything and have all of the answers – that is until it is actually time to get to work. Amazingly, these underperformers usually possess some exceptional skills and abilities, but unfortunately, these attributes are destined to remain untapped, wasted resources. Skills that you have but don't use are worthless. It's like the guy who is an expert auto mechanic who brags about how he can build a muscle car from scratch. However, he refuses to help out or even provide limited guidance with even the smallest tasks. He is worthless – Less Than Zero – because he is a distraction taking up space. But, the willing Novice mechanic who knows just the basics of auto repair but is always willing to pitch in is invaluable. He embodies the Tim Notke truism that **Hard Work Beats Talent when Talent Doesn't Work Hard.**

The rest of the sensible, mature world is very interested in engaging with, working with, or frequently occupying the same space with people who exist on the far end of the achiever's spectrum. Men who successfully tap into their intrinsic energy are driven to compete and achieve, and to be clear, their sexual energy is intertwined with it. This is one of the reasons why it is important for a man to control their sexual urges, until they are on the path to accomplishment (or at least on the path to sincerely coming up with a plan). Men know how to grind hard. They are able to work towards an objective and endure hardship, to reach goals. They minimize distractions and false flags. And, the Nappy Dugout is a false flag; **you can get that quicker than you can get something to eat.** Men also know that if they achieve their goals, every spoil and treat they want, including that Hot(tie) Pocket, will be readily presented to them; they even don't have to go looking for it.

If you're poor, unmotivated, unwilling to at a minimum **TRY**, and lack knowledge or wisdom, you can't provide anybody with anything, aside from conversation and intangibles (which can sometimes be extremely valuable, but I find that happenstance rare). If you fail to initiate the simple ATTEMPT at creating the most basic improvement plan, you prove that you are fundamentally incapable of overcoming even the smallest of obstacles. If you lack the base initiative to act on anything beneficial, you have no Value to those around you, as you are the type who will not pitch in on group work, not cut the overgrown grass, not replace the broken light bulb, not sweep the floor, not clean up the mess YOU made, not repair the broken car, not support your teammates, not work overtime to deliver the critical report, etc. This type of man is essentially a child who relies on others to take care of them, and they are a drain on organizational, community, and familial resources. They hamper business progress, introduce social friction, weaken household cohesion, and degrade interpersonal relationships. If you are a man, make the choice to take control of these critical aspects of your life. All of this is the essence of the formative conversation I had with myself, about My Self, so I know it to be True. There is Iron in these words.

YOU HAVE ALREADY SUCCEEDED

Understand that your optimized Plan, and your success with it, already exists; in order to make manifest this Thing that already is, you have to simply create the proper environment and circumstances, for that Thing that already is, to be revealed. Inside every seed is a full grown plant, but you have to create the proper environment for it to germinate, sprout, ennourish, grow, fend off attack, and mature. This will require paying attention to soil, water, light, nutrients, and our most important resource, Time. **The key to success is to first get started, and then go as fast as you can but not faster than you are capable.** You want to take your time moving in a hurry (Kasdan, 1994). Additionally, you want to take in information and experiences in small, bite-size chunks. Nibble away at the thing you are trying to consume; don't try to choke it all down at once, without proper mastication, as this leads to malabsorption, indigestion, or even rejection. Information modeling can assist with providing an overview of the roadmap your learning will take that can neutralize impatience and keep you on task. For example, my modified version of the DIKW Pyramid (Sharma, 2008):

Hodgerian Rework of the DIKW Pyramid

Datum ➜ **Data** ➜ **Information** ➜ **Mergence** ➜ **Knowledge** ➜ **Comprehension** ➜ **Intelligence** ➜ **Understanding** ➜ **Wisdom** ➜ **Enlightenment.**

Building fiscally sound people is a process that should start early and be habitual. It's never too soon to reply to the kid that says they want McDonald's, by asking them if they mean the food or the stock. This will give you a chance to explain the difference, using something they are already wildly engaged with (I mean, who doesn't like McDonald's – even people who don't like it like it; they really just don't like how much they like it). You can propose an agreement with them, that for every X number of meals they have at McDonald's, they have to buy X amount of McDonald's stock. And, they have to do it with THEIR money — money made from cutting grass, babysitting, or part-time job, for older kids, or from chores around the house, for younger kids.

And how young should you start? I say, as soon as kids start asking for it by name, somewhere between 2-4 years old. Their Ego should begin out-muscling their Id, starting around these ages, as their logical center begins to accelerate development. How do you think the mindset of the 12-year-old who has been buying McDonald's stock for over 6 years and knows they are a shareholder and part owner of one of the most prolific and iconic companies the world has ever seen, might differ from the mindset of the 12-year-old who only eats the burgers? Do you think they might have added some other stocks to their portfolio over the years, based on things they like, using the same agreement? What do you think the impact of this one, easy, exercise will have on their intellectual perspective of the world and how they choose to maneuver through it? Having started at age 5, let's say the 12-year-old has acquired 2 shares of McDonald's stock a year through their own contributions, gifts on birthdays and Christmases, and boons given by grandparents and other family members. Based on September of 2024 prices, that would be 14 total owned shares that result in a total market value of $4,041, providing an annual, passive, dividend income payout of $94. And, that's for a 12-year-old.

NO HATING ON THE ELITE

Now, I understand some of the reasons why you may not have started in the past, on your Money Management, or investment, or leveling up journey. And, I also understand why you don't start now. You're poor, don't have much money, no one has ever given you anything, you don't have enough knowledge, you can't use a computer, you've got bad credit, banks deny your applications for accounts, and life is hard. Boo-Hoo! So what (that's a statement, not a question). **NOBODY CARES.** Get to work getting to work, to make things better for yourself. Most people who accomplish great things weren't given much and did it largely on their own. Depending on which research study you choose, 70% - 85% of all millionaires are self made, started with nothing, and did not inherit money. Most grew up in middle class to poor households. It seems that the saying that if you want the prettiest, healthiest flowers and the largest, strongest trees that bear the most fruit, you've got to dump a lot of Butt Nuggets on them.

The average salary in the U.S. in 2023 was $65,470 (BLS, 2024). That is an insignificant amount of money, for the billionaire class. If we extrapolate that out to the billions, we need to multiply our rounded $65K salary by 1,000,000, resulting in $65 billion or $65,000,000,000. Whew! This also means that if we reverse the logic and divide our $65K salary by 1,000,000, we can see it's non-billionaire equivalent which is $0.065. So, when I say that $65K a year is like pennies to some of those folks, I mean it's like actually pennies - 6 ½ cents, to be exact. Much of society complains about how much money these people have, make, get paid, etc. Although it's certainly no stretch of the imagination to assume that many of the ultra wealthy may be morally compromised and perhaps even criminally inclined, the ratio is also probably not much different than what we would see in the "normal" populace.

If we focus on some of the more well known, modern day billionaires, like Jeff Bezos, Elon Musk, Bill Gates, Mark Zuckerberg, and Warren Buffett, you'll note that there are some interesting tidbits. None of the billionaires in that list got paid cash; it was always stocks and stock options, which means they were essentially betting on themselves to succeed. All of those people were also essentially self-made. I'm sure they may have had mentors, to provide guidance, as well as already established people of means, to stake them, but they were still the captains of their own vessels. And, they all created something revolutionary that society at large benefits from and enjoys, on a daily basis.

Collectively, the companies that they have created, Amazon, Tesla, Microsoft, Meta, and Berkshire Hathaway are currently responsible for creating over **2.4 million direct jobs** (CompaniesMarketCap, 2024). Additionally, the amount of money that flows through them annually is, $1,370,732,000,000, nearly **$1.4 Trillion**. Now, for this flow, I'm not talking about just earnings, or free cash flow, or income. I'm talking about nearly every little piece of actual in and out money movement. I used Operations Activities, Investing Activities, and Financing Activities, from each company's Cash Flow Statement. I then excluded things like Depreciation, Amortization, Goodwill, Intangibles, and Change In Cash, but included things like Accounts Receivables, Tax Payments, Capital Expenditures, Issued Debt, and Repaid Debt. I then totaled it all up, using each line item's absolute value. The absolute value is the key here, as it

disregards positive/negative, converting all integers into whole numbers, which allows the accurate aggregation of the increments. All of that gave me the roughly $1.4 trillion annually number.

This number is important, because of the impact it has beyond the 2.4 million direct jobs provided, as there are also a significant amount of indirect jobs created. There are entire industries that exist to add support services and value added products to what these companies already provide. These jobs and services impact every community, in some fashion. The salaries impact local infrastructure, municipal services, neighborhoods, and the general quality of life, for nearly all Americans, and assumptively, most of the world. The guy that runs the fruit stand keeps 100% of what he generates, after taxes and expenses. However, the billionaire list members keep a much smaller percentage of what the companies that they have created generate.

With all that they have done, how much more do they have to do to justify their wealth? Should earning potential be capped? Perhaps. However, I am conflicted on the notion, due to the amount of power and influence wielded by someone who has unlocked the Billionaire Boss Level. But, capping wealth would be like capping the NBA's Allen Iverson, every time he scored 25 points; he could keep playing, but his made shots would no longer count. This would negatively impact Iverson's value, as a facilitator and distributor, and create an inferior product for the audience and consumers. So, I guess the better and more relevant question is, what have you done to try to make the world better, even if you sometimes get it wrong, like the billionaires do? And, better than even that, what have you done for your immediate family and those you say you care about? No, I don't want to hate on the elite. With luck not withstanding, I want to figure out what they have done and are doing to be successful and try to replicate some of that success.

ESTATE PLANNING

Another resource to address, at a somewhat early age, is the Estate Plan. I personally believe that by the time kids are in high school, at the latest, the Estate Plan should be discussed. If you are the parent, I think it wise to discuss some of what your intentions are for your Estate Plan, how it was created, how everything works, what your intentions are, how you want them to handle your legacy, etc. Someone who was trained, since childhood, on how to best manage a family heritage is going to be much more effective at executing on the parent's vision, than someone who is unschooled. And, I think it also makes sense to have the young adult entertain creating their own plan, as well. After all, this is no typical young adult – they have assets. They own stuff, because a thoughtful parent has had them buying stock, since they were 5 years old.

Most people create a simple Will, for their Estate Plan. Personally, I prefer the **Revocable Living Trust** (as opposed to the Irrevocable Living Trust). The difference between these is that a Will takes effect after a person dies, while a Living Trust is in effect while a person is alive and typically includes things like cars, real estate, bank accounts, investment accounts, etc., along with its identifying the beneficiaries. The Irrevocable Living Trust is just that, meaning you can't make changes to it, once it is established. But, the Revocable Living Trust allows you to make changes. It also skips probate court, remains private, and Trust assets transfer immediately. However, if you think you'll be making a lot of changes, need the mediation of probate, or have a child guardianship obligation, then you will still need a Will (and yes, it's OK to have both a Will and a Living Trust).

Regardless of the solution(s) you choose, it is critically important for your family that you complete this task. That's what responsible, grown folks do. If you have assets, consider yourself smart, and proclaim to have buckets of affection for your family, but you do not have an estate plan, your family may be unwillingly forced to forfeit your assets. This means you are actually not that smart after all. And, perhaps you don't even have that much genuine affection for your family, in any capacity, if you can't even take the time to construct a simple, minimalist Will.

PSYCHOLOGY & PHYSIOLOGY

Nearly every undertaking you embark on holds the bulk of what makes you successful at it, as mental currency. Everything is a mind game. The practical and physical execution is important, for sure. But, the thing that really ensures your best chance at being successful at any undertaking is the combination of your psychological approach, intellectual discipline, and mental outlook. Personal Money Management is not unique in this regard. Two areas of understanding that can help you take control of these psychological impacts are the **Freudian Psychic Apparatus**, consisting of the Id, Ego, and Superego (Freud, 1922) and the prime movers of your body's pleasure centers, consisting of **dopamine, oxytocin, serotonin, and endorphin** (Mountainside, n.d.).

The Freudian Psychic Apparatus consists of the Id, Ego, and Superego. Sigmund Freud – the man who was once deemed unfit for a Nobel Prize, based on his work being scientifically worthless – is a controversial figure to this day (Branchereau, 2017). Although many of Freud's theories have over time been dubiousized, and many proven completely wrong, I still find his Psychic Apparatus an excellent, heuristic tool to use in real world

applications. I often compare it to how, in the Information Technology sphere, we use the OSI Model to aid in understanding and troubleshooting computer networks, even though the TCP/IP Model is what's in practical use. The Freudian Psychic Apparatus aspects are pure psychology and do not correspond to any somatic structures in the brain. For instance, there is no physical part of the brain where you can say that, "the Id is physically located here", or that, "the Superego can be found there". The Id is primal need fulfillment, sexual energy, and desire. The Superego is focused on perfection, idealism, and fantasy. The Ego is the logical and reasoning aspect that acts as a buffer and liaison between the Id and the Superego.

We'll briefly discuss these concepts further, later in the book, but here is how you can use them as tools to help with your decisioning or discipline. Make a pact with yourself that for the next item you are passionate about acquiring that you will first research the thing and also list the pros and cons associated with its acquisition. Determine which aspect of the Psychic Apparatus you think is dominant within you, as you finalize your decision. It should be the Ego, your logical aspect. Then, for the next impulse purchase you are on the cusp of actually making, stop before you swipe your card, hand over cash, or click the button to buy. Again, determine which aspect you think is dominant. It will probably be the Id. Try to hold off on that purchase, until you feel the Ego is once again dominant. Finally, in the next disagreement you have or tense meeting you're getting ready to attend, make a determination on which aspect you believe is dominant within you. If your Ego is not clearly in control, use **4-4-4 Combat Breathing** to regain control; take a 4-second breath in, hold it for 4-seconds, and then exhale for 4-seconds. Reassess. Repeat as necessary.

For the second scenario, before crossing the threshold into any arena where there is going to be contention, force the Ego to the front just as you approach the threshold's demarcation. Once you enter the theater (lobby, chat, conference room, video teleconference, classroom, etc.), try to also assess what aspect you think is dominant in each of the participants. Reassess them, as well as yourself, throughout the engagement. Knowing which aspect is dominant in an adversary is critical to determining which tools are most effective against them. For example, attempting to reason with someone who is unreasonable, due to their severe Id or Superego dominance, is ineffective. Learn to assess, and use the correct tool for the job you have before you. And, bear in mind that you will need to employ these tactics against yourself most of the time, as most of us are rarely in full control of our desires, wants, and needs. This masturbatory, cerebral exercise becomes essential for our optimized decision-making. We often don't even recognize that we're not in control, as **Id Bleed** and **Superego Drift** create distracting, logical quagmires that add psychological noise, impacting our ability to effectively reason. Recursive analysis is the salve for these ailments. For our pleasure centers, however, the approach is markedly different.

I have heard it said that, "Money can't buy happiness", and I agree with that. **Money might not be able to buy happiness, but it can rent it.** And, you can CERTAINLY buy a whole heck of a lot of pleasure with it. Having abundant resources to leverage the Pleasure Principle can be the soothing ointment for much of what ails us. But, THAT is the crux of a major misidentification. We ignorantly intertwine happiness and pleasure, treating them as one and the same, when they are entirely different things. Pleasure is the resultant, short term, biochemical sledgehammer that's made to violently energize and propel you. Happiness is the long-term blanket that is made to nimbly provide sustained, network-wide vigor. They can synergistically feed off one another, as well as impact one another, sometimes negatively. For example, too much pleasure may reduce your happiness, due to biochemical signaling conflicts. Although our bodies may produce additional happy/pleasure elements, I will focus on dopamine, serotonin, oxytocin, and endorphin. Similar to how you can't use Ego tools to drastically impact the Id, you can't use pleasure tools to drastically impact happiness and vice versa. So what's the difference?

Well, we run into problems when we are seeking happiness but use pleasure mechanisms to achieve it. That will never work. They use completely different physiological pathways. Dopamine and serotonin are neurotransmitters, while oxytocin and endorphin are hormones. Neurotransmitters operate within the nervous system, are transmitted via the synaptic cleft, impact areas in its immediate vicinity, and typically respond within milliseconds. Hormones operate within the endocrine system, are transmitted via blood, impact areas far from where they were produced, and take minutes to days to respond. One distinction between the things that make you happy and the things that bring you pleasure is that you can take a substance or do something and immediately feel pleasure, but happiness comes on a bit slower, over a longer period of time. And, long after the mercurial hit of pleasure has passed (seconds to minutes to hours), the growing warmth of happiness continues to intensify (hours to days to weeks).

Also, due to the phenomenon of **hedonic adaptation** (Scott, 2022), a person will typically return to some type of stasis, regardless of how high or low they were. Too much pleasure seeking eventually leads to addiction, as receptors are downregulated. We always try to return to normal, but when the abnormal becomes normalized, it becomes the new normal, and biochemically, we treat it as such. If the crest amplitude of pleasure is exceedingly high, the corresponding valley trough will eventually match it, as it seeks equilibrium, essentially crashing after a high. I find that existing within a moderate range is best for me. I know that if I remain grounded, intelligent, and disciplined, I at least have a chance to persevere through most of what life throws at me. I don't want to get too high or excited, or too low or depressed. Tangentially, stocks similarly have a hedonic adaptation type of action called Mean Reversion, where a stock's price tends to return to its average price, over time.

Ultimately, what all of this means is that effective Money Management and investing are intellectual and emotional pursuits where those who exhibit discipline, patience, and sound logic tend to thrive the most. Sure, there are those who have thrown caution to the wind, went out on a limb, captured lightning in a bottle, pulled a royal flush, grabbed the golden ticket, and won the lottery (I'm out of clichés here, but you get the point), but those occurrences are rare. Also, for the ones fortunate enough to be granted a bounty, do they possess the skills and disposition to keep it, or better yet, thrive with it? Together, let us figure out how to thrive, regardless of what our means and circumstances are.

LIVE LIKE YOUR LIFE DEPENDS ON IT

Hopefully, you've set a goal to improve some aspect of your life. And here, we say that a goal is where the Value of the pursuit and attainment of a thing outweighs the resource allocation detriment and sacrifice required to achieve it. But, achieving meaningful goals is not easy (very few things that are worthwhile are). When learning new things, **be OK with not being OK**. You're going to make mistakes. And, not only is that acceptable, it's to be expected. If you're doing it right, you will keep making mistakes, because you're always accepting new challenges and trying to learn new things. Adopting the Right mindset is the only prep work you really need to get started with ANYTHING! Having the Right mindset is akin to framing a house before erecting the walls, creating the mold before casting the image, or writing the script before filming the movie. I mean, you can embark on all of those without doing the prerequisites, but any successes will be luck and most likely unrepeatable.

To restate a notion from "The Strangest Secret", the Earl Nightingale masterpiece, if a farmer has fertile, conditioned land, that land doesn't care what is planted on it (Nightingale, 1956/2006). Here, the land and the human brain are equivalencies. From a practical perspective, it's important to note that your brain is not your friend.

Your Brain Has 3 Core Tasks:

1. **Protect the host.**
2. **Administer and run the environment.**
3. **Provide feedback, and record conscious and unconscious phenomena.**

(Hodge, 2019)

Your brain is impersonally duty bound, and just because it's yours, it doesn't mean it's looking out for your best interests, in all cases. In Earl Nightingale's notion, the land operates the same way as our brains do. It simply returns whatever is planted, whether that be **produce or poison.** Each person's lifetime is like a plot of land. Each of us has been given a plot, and everyone's plot is a little different; plots may be hilly, flat, rocky, fertile, barren, frozen, muddy, pest infested, wooded, etc. and on and on. Irregardless (heh), everyone is given a plot. Some people who are given meager plots are industrious, work their land, and do great things with it. Some are given exceptional plots, full of potential, and do absolutely nothing with it at all. Some are jealous of other people's plots, even though they have done little of substance to improve their own. And some are inspired by others' plots of land and seek personal excellence by following their examples. Regardless of the plot of land you were given and the circumstances surrounding it, the choice is yours on what you do with it. You have a choice on whether to plant the kindred seeds of resentment, jealousy, discontentment, malice, etc. or to plant the kindred seeds of determination, fellowship, honor, integrity, and its ilk. It's your Plot of Land, after all. Heeding the Call to Adventure and embarking on your individual, terrestrial **Hero's Journey** is unavoidable. Delinquency is not an option. And, after your Ordeals, Transformation, and Return, you don't have to tell anybody about how well you tended your land, or what kind of farmer you were, or what kind of seeds you planted; everybody can already tell all of that, by the types of crops on, and the condition of – **Your Plot of Land**.

SO, WHAT IS THE ANABOLIC APPROACH?

I'm an Artist and Systems Engineer by nature and by design, so my first instinct is to solve problems. Different people would approach me about their money woes, and I would try to answer the questions I was being asked or create solutions for the problems I was being presented. I progressed from having conversations about Money Management, to advocating for fantasy investing, to creating documents on basics, to delivering presentations on How-Tos – Few Takers. I escalated by gifting start up money, so people could get some real world experience, on my dime. They would be using real money, on real systems, in real markets, in

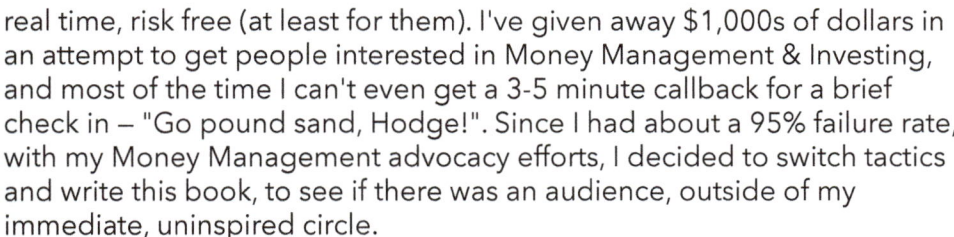

real time, risk free (at least for them). I've given away $1,000s of dollars in an attempt to get people interested in Money Management & Investing, and most of the time I can't even get a 3-5 minute callback for a brief check in – "Go pound sand, Hodge!". Since I had about a 95% failure rate, with my Money Management advocacy efforts, I decided to switch tactics and write this book, to see if there was an audience, outside of my immediate, uninspired circle.

But, I needed a hook. And, I had the perfect candidate, since I also frequently fielded questions about strength training and nutrition. I had started lifting heavy weights in college but was more of a powerlifter than bodybuilder – I wanted to **BE** strong and powerful, and not just **LOOK** strong and powerful. I also had been a personal trainer for years, as well as the General Manager for several gyms (Gold's, Powerhouse, World, and a few others), so I know the strength game well. Melding my financial approach with strength training principles was my hook. Hence, Fisicality and its Anabolic Approach was created.

Simply put, the Anabolic Approach is the mixing and leveraging of the parallels between the Money Management & Investing world and the Fitness & Strength Training world. The similarities these two distinct areas have has always tickled the back of my brain. If you can invest successfully, you can be a formidable strength athlete. If you can lift heavy stuff, you can be a bullet-proof investor. **It's the same skill set, applied to a different activity.** They both require discipline, research, planning, tracking, toughness, and resiliency. In order to participate, you have to put your own resources at risk, and miscalculations or undesirable outcomes could result in you experiencing immediate and direct pain and loss (similar to that of a fighter). And, the ultimate shared characteristic is that both require consistency for long stretches of time, with no guarantee of a desirable outcome. Growth comes slowly, sometimes imperceptibly so, and it may even stall out or regress, but you are required to push on, just to have a chance at receiving the potential, long-term reward. Lazily, languidly, and lethargically, pennies turn into dollars, and ounces turn into pounds (heh). It takes the same fundamental approach and fortitude, to succeed at both of these endeavors. One is mostly intellectual, requiring only modest physical effort, while the other is mostly physical, requiring only modest intellectual effort. However, these two disparate worlds exhibit a remarkable harmony. They wholly align, due to the mental effort required (mental and intellectual are not the same thing). And, the mental requirement for excellence is staggering. It is punishment. You must be, all kinds of ways, resilient, strong, and powerful, to excel at this work (and at anything else of substance, for that matter). **Strength is being able to take punishment; Power is being able to deliver it.**

FISICALITY

SECTION 2

BOARDING

Adopt the Right Mindset

Success is Determined at the Beginning

It may not seem like it, but your disposition at this very moment is what will give you the best chance at being successful. Obtaining and maintaining the proper mindset is a precursor to performing well. Your brain can't distinguish between visualizing success and actual success. Intensely visualizing success strengthens the neural pathways associated with a selected scenario.

DID YOU KNOW?

The Average Person Has

50
THOUSAND
Thoughts Per Day
Only 2500 Are New

Widely attributed to the National Science Foundation, but no supporting academic papers found.

MOTIVATION   **DISCIPLINE**   **DETERMINATION**

MOTIVATION

What are your reasons for getting started? What are your reasons for **NOT** getting started? Do you become energized simply thinking about the project? Are you as excited about the **process** of achieving your goals, as you are the **prospect** of achieving your goals.

DISCIPLINE

Do you possess the internal grit to follow through? Can you focus on **The Work**? Do you frequently set goals only to abandon them, shortly after engaging? Do you have reoccurring goals that never track towards completion? Can you maintain focus and overcome distractions?

DETERMINATION

Are you willing to **suffer** to reach your goals? Can you fight for what you say you want, by yourself, with no support system, and perhaps even **people close to you actively plotting against you**? Are you willing to sacrifice your wants and restrict needs to work towards your goals?

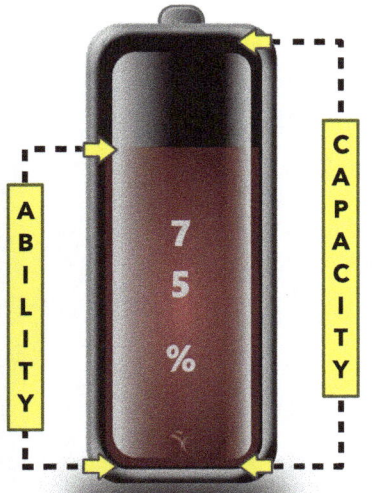

Capacity & Ability

Know the difference between Capacity and Ability, and be mindful of it. Capacity is Inherent Effectiveness under optimal conditions. Ability is Situational Effectiveness, given available resources, under existing, point-in-time conditions.

Do not make promises about your Ability, based on your Capacity.

There Is No Right Way To Do The Wrong Thing

There IS a better way to do the Wrong Thing. And, there is an effective way, an efficient way, and even an optimal way to do the Wrong Thing. But, there is no Right way to do it. Oftentimes, many of us experience great success in our endeavors and subsequently are comforted by the spoils provided by that success. However, it is critical that we maintain clarity in knowing that the things we are good at and successful at doing are actually also the Right things to be doing. Lack of understanding around these concepts is a surefire way to achieve a goal, yet still feel unsatisfied and unfulfilled. It is only when your Actions align with what you say you're all about that you are able to exploit the energy created by Conviction.

When I Say I Want To Get Some McDonald's and a Coke, I'm Not Talking About Just The Food

Don't get me wrong. I like the food – a lot. There is very little that can compete with a Big Mac with six patties, a perfectly cooked order of golden, meaty fries, and an ice cold Coke, with just enough ice in it to create the perfect amount of dilution and crispness. But, when I say, "I want some McDonald's", most of the time, I'm talking about stock in the company. If I own stock in the company, every time I eat a Big Mac, I'm paying myself, just a little bit, to eat it. Pairing McDonald's stock with Coke stock is a one-two punch, since they are essentially a packaged deal in the restaurants. I benefit from the significant overlap, synergy, and substantial fiscal moat they collectively have.

Foundational Data

Goals and Objectives should simply and clearly state what you are trying to do. The importance of the notion of "simply" cannot be understated, for this next step.

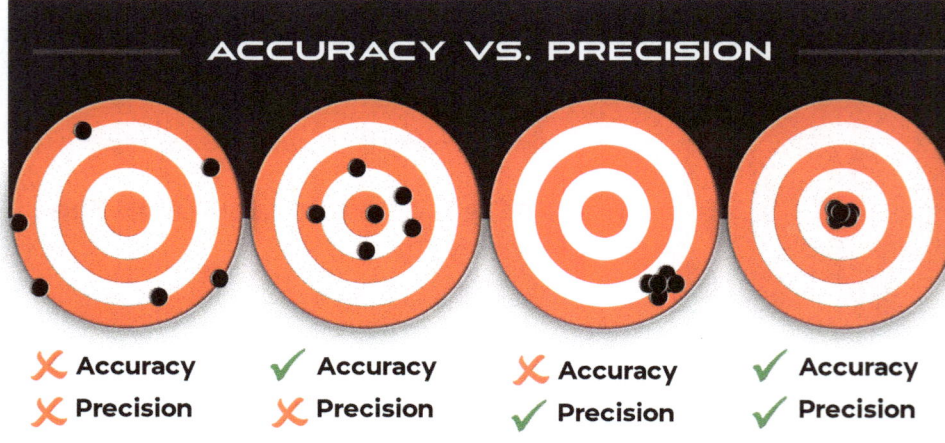

ACCURACY VS. PRECISION

✗ Accuracy ✓ Accuracy ✗ Accuracy ✓ Accuracy
✗ Precision ✗ Precision ✓ Precision ✓ Precision

Accuracy is how close the results are to the goal; Precision is how close the results are to each other. You MUST, at all costs, be Accurate, before being Precise.

There is a big difference between taking Calculated Risks and being Reckless. Too often, poorly thought-out initiatives are embarked upon, only to be justified with hackneyed phrases and platitudes. Somewhere along the way, folks figure out that they have been very Precise, as they have over analyzed meaningless minutiae ad nauseam, but they haven't been very Accurate, because they've been aiming at the wrong targets. In terms of an **Accepted Value** (AV), results that are close to the AV are Accurate, while results that are consistently reproducible, even if distant from the AV, are Precise.

So, this means that Accuracy is about being correct or within a known specification, while Precision is about exactness or being repeatable. A gross example that shows the validity of this assertion that you must FIRST be accurate at all costs would be an All-Star point guard hitting 10 out 10 3-point shots, in a single game (which is Precise), but making the last 3-pointer, with the game tied, at the buzzer, in the opponent's net (which is not Accurate).

VISION
(The Perfect Trip Defined)
This is the fantasy. It may be influenced by later stage Improvements. [May start with the verb "Become" to target the future.]

MISSION
(Reason for Travel)
This is the reason for existing or seeking the Vision. [May start with the preposition "To" to indicate purpose.]

GOAL
(Destination)
This is the Big Idea. It is represented as a vague, malleable Outcome Statement. Leverage Adam Kreek's CLEAR Formula.

OBJECTIVES
(Way Points)
These are the Little Ideas that leverage George Doran's SMART Formula, in their construction.

STRATEGIES
(The Compass)
These are the Methods of Operating, Plans of Action, and Guidelines to follow when implementing Tactics.

TACTICS
(Map & Vehicle Utilization)
These are the actual Tools and specific Methods used to achieve the Objectives in accordance with the Strategies.

TASKS
(The Movement)
These are the actual, specific Actions taken to realize the Tactics, in accordance with the Strategies.

ANALYSIS
(Route and Time Inspection)
This is the Tactic-Specific measurement tracking and the review of results.

IMPROVEMENTS
(Route, Time, and Task Modifications)
These are the analysis-based adjustments.

DECOMMISSION
(Post Trip Actions)
Part of planning a new implementation is also creating the plan and timetable for its decommission, before it is even birthed.

ACCURACY DECREASES

PRECISION DECREASES

(Hodge, 2019)

HODGERIAN ACTION MODEL

I won't go into much detail reviewing the chart to the left, aside from saying it's my interpretation of the correct order for achieving goals and satisfying objectives. But, I will go into great detail on it in another work, in the near future. I have attempted to definitively describe the Nature, Scope, and Function of the thing. For our purposes, we will focus primarily on the practical aspects, the two most important of which are the Goal and Objective sections.

BITE-SIZE PIECES AND ITERATIONS

From my perspective, I find that there is no better way to consistently take meaningful action and measurably track towards achieving an objective than to break it down into bite size pieces, consume it, and then continuously loop through the process. This allows you to experience the satisfaction and dopamine rush of accomplishing something on a regular basis, while also enjoying the benefits gained from actually progressing toward your destination, in a meaningful, real-world way.

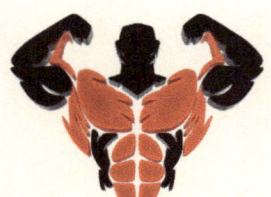

The Anabolic Approach Explained

Fiscal & Physical Alignment

Bodybuilders, powerlifters, crossfitters, strength athletes, weekend warriors, and home gym heroes are all well suited to fiscal investment endeavors. I'd go so far as to say that they may be the class of individuals most well suited to excel, when it comes to managing money and investing. Strength athletes live in a world where **extreme discomfort** (that they have purposely caused) is the norm. And, it occurs consistently for days, weeks, months, and even years, at a time. Additionally, there is no guarantee of reward, there is significant risk of injury, and pleasure, short term enjoyment, and even life essentials are often sacrificed, for their work. Whether engaged in basketball, football, mixed martial arts, swimming, volleyball, rugby, ping-pong, or a host of other pursuits, the athletes who excel at weightlifting, usually perform at a higher level than those who don't. Adding weight training can make a good athlete great and a great athlete exceptional. For example, Tiger Woods revolutionized golf, in 1997, not only due to his technical skill but also his use of weight training to improve strength, flexibility, and balance, which increased his driving power.

The approach it takes to be successful in strength training is the exact same approach it takes to be successful in Money Management. Anabolic athletes and investors are the perfect pair. They both require ample-to-excessive **motivation, discipline, and determination,** to be successful. And, they both require constant activity monitoring of ability and capability, to ensure consistent progress, without experiencing setbacks.

In many cases, strength athletes place themselves in harm's way, as a normal part of their regimen. Three or four hundred pounds, pressed at arms length, on a bench press, is enough to seriously injure or kill, if mishandled, but these athletes do that and more on a regular basis. They are not only physically strong, they are also mentally tough and resilient. Similarly, the investor may place a significant percentage of their wealth at risk and do so on a regular basis, and that also requires mental toughness and resilience. Simultaneously engaging in both activities results in significant, synergistic benefits.

Money Set

_____

_____

_____

_____

_____

_____

_____

_____

_____

_____

_____

Gary Player

won 9 regular golfing majors. He used **FORCED REPS & DROP SETS** weight training to add over 30 yards to his driving distance, in 1 year, and won his first PGA Masters Tournament, in 1961.

(Kerr-Dineen, 2023)

Visionary

Player was truly ahead of his time, as even the NFL didn't see its first dedicated, strength coach hire, until 1963, with the San Diego Chargers bringing Alvin Roy on board. Gary Player had already been lifting heavy weights, since the 1950s, by that time.

(The Football Odyssey, 2020)

The OODA Loop

The OODA Loop (Boyd, 1995) began its development in 1951 by former U.S. Air Force fighter pilot, John Boyd. The acronym stands for: Observe, Orient, Decide, Act. Boyd developed it as an attempt to define a system to optimize aerial dogfighting performance. The pilots who could repeatedly travel the loop the quickest had the best chance of being successful. The OODA Loop is simultaneously a system for learning, a framework for dealing with uncertainty, and a strategy to victory, in a direct combat situation. I find this such a simple, elegant, and practical tool for getting desired results in the real world, and I have used it many times in sticky situations. It helps you keep your wits about you, calms you down, and forces you to focus on working The Loop.

If you can commit and be consumed by it under duress, you'll find yourself more focused on and distracted by The Loop, as opposed to being more focused on and consumed by fear and panic. We can also employ OODA Loop thought and techniques, within our Money Management program.

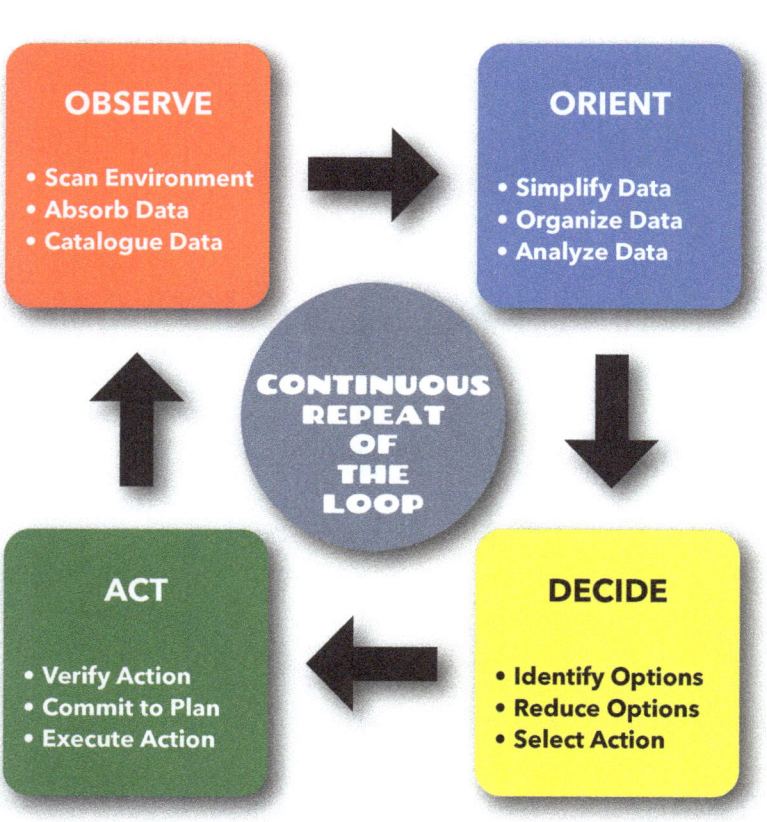

Repeat The Loop with the knowledge gained from each cycle. Preceding cycles become input and data for subsequent iterations of The Loop.

Knowledge derived from practical action is now experience. Your experience will grow, and you will become more **efficient** with Observation and Orientation and more **proficient** with Deciding and Acting, with each subsequent pass through The Loop.

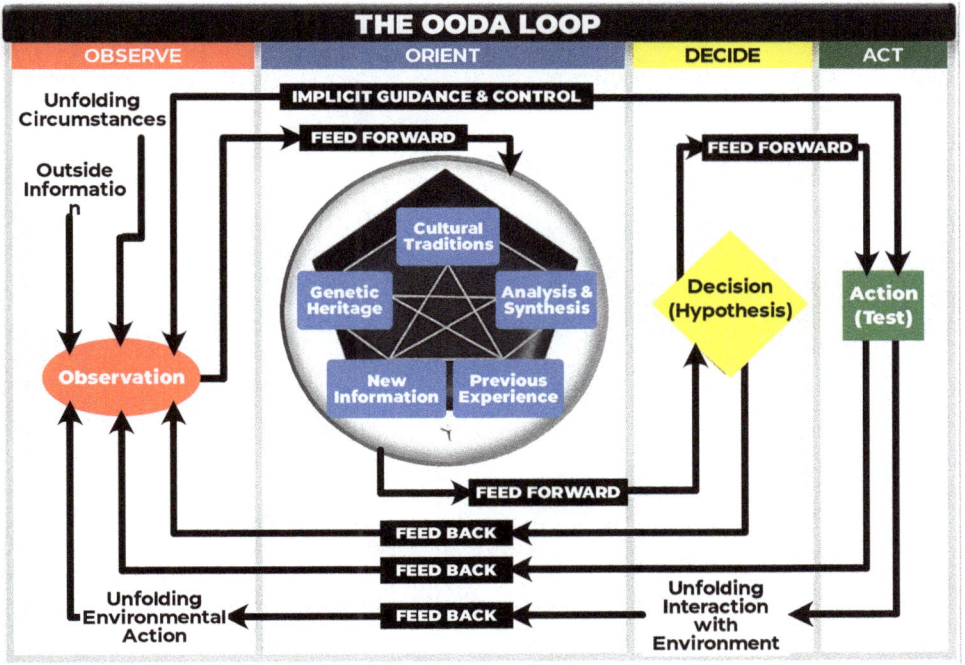

(Hodge, 2019)

1. **Observe** – Analyze our current state. Are we getting the results we want out of our job, relationships, and life, in general? Would more money improve our situation? Can we simulate making more money by managing what we currently have better? Before sacrificing things we actually want to keep or acquire, are there waste items we could eliminate to salvage losses?

2. **Orient** – What is the expected level of effort? Can we commit to the endeavor? What tools are available to optimize the effort? What can we do immediately to get started? What is most important and what is least important? What can be sacrificed, with minimal impact?

3. **Decide** – What does logic say is the prudent course of action? What does experience suggest? What does our gut say to do? Make a decision.

4. **Act** – Do what you have planned and decided. Execute.

Stop Thinking, Just Act

Lot's of folks have lots of I'm-plannings, and I'm-gonnas, and, I'm-thinking-ofs, and I'm-finnuhs, but they do nothing. Once you have taken the time to plan and have decided on a course of action, TAKE THAT ACTION!

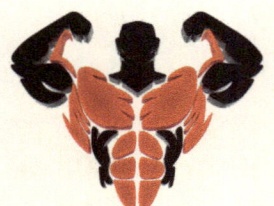

The Anabolic Approach Explained

The OODA Loop for Weightlifters

On the Money Management side, typical OODA Loop cycle traversal is slower (hours, days, and weeks) than it is on the Anabolic side (seconds, minutes, minutes, and hours), unless there is an emergency, or you are day trading. In this example, note that the Anabolic Athlete constantly cycles through the OODA Loop, during every workout.

OBSERVE - They look at the workout area, check the environmental temperature, determine the crowd and congestion levels, check for existing muscle soreness, determine their mental state and level of motivation, and mentally stage the planned routine for the day.

ORIENT - They take all of the information listed above, and more, to construct mental models, of their workout, that explore the best exercises to do, the order in which to do them, and the planned effort.

DECIDE - Based on the Orientation Result, they select a mental model.

ACT - They begin their workout, using the selected model.

Here is where the magic happens. The workout goes through The Loop, and so does every set, and so does every rep. The bodybuilder is iteratively cycling through Observe-Orient-Decide-Act, FOR EVERY SINGLE REP. He is making micro adjustments, on rep cadence, movement depth, joint angle, and muscle squeeze, as he goes. Then, the same cycle is also occurring at a Workout Set level. Four sets may have been planned, but if he's feeling diesel on this day, another couple of sets, using more weight, get added. Or, conversely, if he felt a destructive twinge on the last rep of the previous set, he will end the exercise there, and attempt a workaround. At the workout level, the previous workout session acts as data input for the next workout's OODA Loop and is used to assist in making adjustments. If there was a significant strength increase during the previous workout, the current workout's weight targets or intensity may be adjusted to account for those previous, real-world levels, instead of what the designed program called for. Weightlifters are masters of The OODA Loop.

Money Set

_____
_____
_____
_____
_____
_____
_____
_____
_____
_____
_____
_____

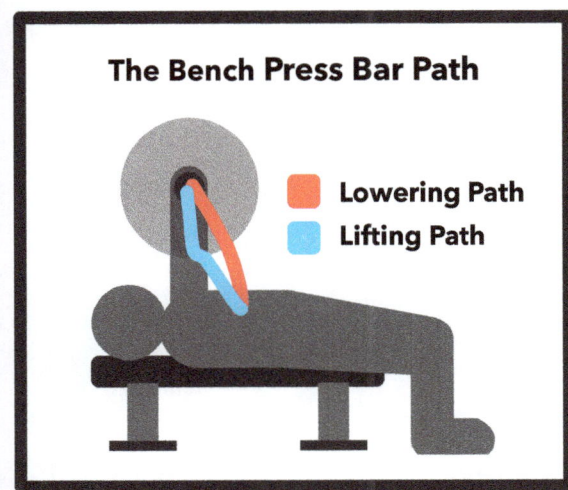

The Bench Press Bar Path

🟧 Lowering Path
🟦 Lifting Path

The Lifting Path, for heavy Bench Pressing, is not straight up and down. On the **descent**, it is an arc. On the **ascent**, the lifter pushes back towards their head and then straight up. Lifters constantly make micro-adjustments to the path, speed, and angle during every rep.

(Nuckols, n.d.)

Creating the Master Repository

Primary Site and Off-Site Repositories

You should establish a Primary Site and an Off-Site Repository. The Primary Site Repo is simply what you'll be using on a daily basis, to manage your money. The Off-Site Repo(s) is a frequently updated copy of data stored at the Primary Site. While some of the data can be somewhat stale, the authentication data need to updated immediately.

Consolidated Data

Data 1   Data 2   Data 3
Data collected from multiple sources are aggregated into a single authoritative resource.

(FILE)

> **MONEY . . . IS A TERRIBLE MASTER, BUT AN EXCELLENT SERVANT.**
>
> – P.T. BARNUM
> (Barnum, 1888/2023)

Primary Site Admin

The Authoritative Data are loaded, for direct administration.
(COMPUTER)

Primary Site Secure Storage

Updated Authoritative Data are securely archived at the Primary Site.
(SAFE)

CONSIDERATIONS

For redundancy, I find it wise to have both an analogue and digital copy of my repository, in my on-site and off-site locations. Things to watch out for with the analogue method is the kind of paper, ink, and moisture control used. Freshly printed documents that are sealed in a waterproof, airtight container will almost certainly fall victim to spoilage, due to mold and mildew. Periodic document reviews and document lamination can help with this, but it's not a set it and forget it solution.

Off-Site 1 Secure Storage

Updated Authoritative Data are replicated Off-Site.
(CLOUD)

Off-Site 2 Secure Storage

Updated Authoritative Data are replicated Off-Site.
(BANK)

Physical Media Longevity

For the digital solution, be aware of the limitations of your off-site storage media. For example, DVD+R DL has a stable longevity of 5-10 years, while a CD-R that uses phthalocyanine dye with a gold metal layer has an expected stable longevity of over 100 years. Similarly, hard drives are subject to data fade and bit rot, SSDs are also vulnerable to data fade, primarily when they are not powered which prevents them from executing their normal refresh operations.

Newer JEDEC compliant SSDs are required to retain data for 365 days when powered off and stored at 30 degrees Celsius. Keep in mind, this is for new SSDs that have not exhausted many of their

Program/Erase cycles. Drives that have been heavily used will likely not meet the standard and will fail prematurely. Thumb and flash drives are similar to SSDs. With these drives, it is important to eject them safely, rather than just yanking them out of the active port.

These are just some of the more readily accessible digital storage options, but more robust methods, such as M-Disc, exist at a premium cost. Well, actually an M-Disc solution doesn't cost that much, and it has a projected lifespan of 1000 years. The recommendation here is to do what you can, with what you have, where you are now, and upgrade later, as your situation and resources allow.

(M-Disk, 2019)

(Canadian Conservation institute, 2020)

STORAGE LONGEVITY

SOLUTION	YEARS	EFFORT
BD-R (dye or non-dye, single layer or dual layer)	5 - 10	Low
DVD-RW (erasable DVD)	5 - 10	Low
DVD+R DL (dual layer)	5 - 10	Low
BD-R (non-dye, gold metal layer)	10 - 20	Low
DVD-R (silver alloy metal layer)	10 - 20	Low
DVD and BD (read-only, such as a DVD or Blu-ray movie)	10 - 20	Low
CD-RW (erasable CD)	20 - 50	Low
BD-RE (erasable Blu-ray)	20 - 50	Low
DVD+R (silver alloy metal layer)	20 - 50	Low
CD-R (cyanine or azo dye, silver alloy metal layer)	20 - 50	Low
DVD+RW (erasable DVD)	20 - 50	Low
CD-R (phthalocyanine dye, silver alloy metal layer)	50 - 100	Low
CD (read-only, such as an audio CD)	50 - 100	Low
CD-R (phthalocyanine dye, gold metal layer)	100	Low
JEDEC Compliant SSD	1	Medium
Hard Drive	3 - 5	Medium
Flash Drive	1	Medium
LTO Tape	30	High

Analogue and Digital Repository Security

IT Security revolves around an Asset-Threat-Vulnerability Matrix. The 3 elements in this matrix must be constantly weighed against each other to create the optimum solution, for any point in time.

Even if a password is very secure from cracking attacks, it may not be secure from a retrievability perspective. I mean, if you can't remember it, have to write it down, and then store it somewhere close by, it's only as secure as what you wrote it down on and where you stored it. It's safe from the digital world (mostly) but not from the analogue world.

And, if you decided to print it out, well your printer is a computer also. How secure is that printer? Some printers have hard drives, non-volatile memory, network connections to external apps, etc. Any of these could be an infiltration point for a threat actor.

But, getting back to the super duper password itself, a passphrase can provide the same protection AND give you the ability to easily remember it. And, if you mate your well crafted passphrase to a password manager that creates complex passwords for all of your other resources, as well, you will have a reasonably secure solution.

Of course, all of this is contingent upon you cultivating good security habits and maintaining discipline. Putting all of these heightened security measures and best practices into place, only to violate protocol at a critical point, breaks the whole paradigm. For example, 50 character resource passwords can be rendered moot, by having a weak Password Vault Password that puts the whole program in jeopardy.

MFA

Multi-Factor Authentication should be used whenever possible. Use the most robust, supported authentication method you have available for your resource, as a rule. If you have a choice between a lesser MFA method and no MFA, choose the lesser MFA Method, as it will still provide Defense-in-Depth.

50 CHARACTERS
My minimum password length, when available.

RECOMMENDATIONS

To simplify management and ensure adherence to long, random passwords, I recommend using a password manager. For the multifactor component, I recommend mating the password with a hardware based security key. Finally, if your vendor offers an option to use a passkey, consider using it.

Many Banks Are Underspec'd

Interestingly, banks, which house some of your most critical assets, fall way behind in the options they offer to secure your accounts. This means you must be extra careful and not make any mistakes with them. Some of our largest banks and trading platforms currently only offer username, password, SMS, and Symantec VIP Access. Support for authenticator

Printers Are Rarely Secure

▶ Document Theft
▶ Shoulder Surfing
▶ Plaintext Data
▶ Stored Data
▶ Settings Modifications
▶ Network Attacks

apps, passphrases, and hardware keys is sorely lacking. According to Statista, there were over 61 million victims of financial data breaches, in the United States alone, in 2023. Couple this with their assertion that 40% of U.S adults are likely to fall victim to financial cybercrime, and you start to better understand the full scope and impact of weak security countermeasures.
(Petrosyan, 2024)

Device Vulnerability Percentages

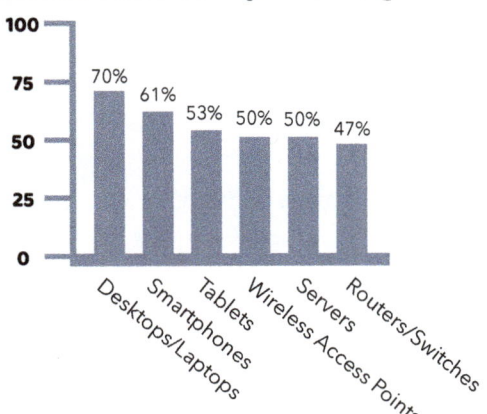

Leading Malware Carriers

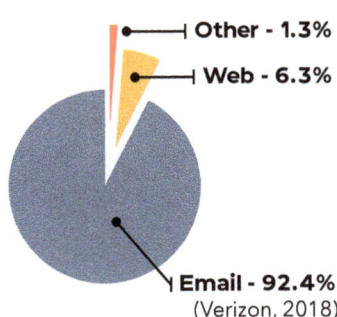

Other - 1.3%
Web - 6.3%
Email - 92.4%
(Verizon, 2018)

PROTECT YOUR DEVICES
Worldwide, smartphones comprise **60%** of internet traffic, AND **61%** of smartphones are vulnerable to attack. The exposure factor of this one element is massive. (GilPress, 2024)

EMAIL SAFETY IS CRITICAL
Email is responsible for a whopping **92%** of all malware payloads in all circumstances. Ensuring proper protocols and habits, when using email, is particularly impactful. From a practical use perspective, email is frequently used as a primary identification source and communications method for nearly all of our sensitive and critical accounts. Protect it!

The Anabolic Approach Explained

The Asset-Threat-Vulnerability (ATV) Matrix

Olympic lifting is arguably one of the single most demanding sports there is. At its core, it simply involves the lifter raising a plate-loaded barbell from the floor to overhead. That's it. To make things even simpler, there are really only 2 lifts, the Snatch and the Clean & Jerk. The Snatch is where the lifter grabs the bar with a wide grip and raises it overhead in a single, fluid motion that usually results in the lifter ending up in the overhead squat position, before they stand up with the weight, still overhead, to complete the lift – brutal. The Clean & Jerk is no less involved, but it essentially starts from and ends in the same positions as The Snatch. To be successful, in either lift, an athlete needs exceptional strength, functional power (strength and power are not the same thing), precise coordination, good balance, controlled explosiveness, excellent technique, durability to maintain form, and mental toughness.

The Olympic Lifter must constantly engage ATV. The collective **Asset** is the athlete and their ability to perform the lift. **Threats** could be internal or external to the athlete, such as their having a lack of access to quality food, having a lack of competent coaching, or enduring long, day job, work hours. **Vulnerabilities** would be current weakness in core areas, such as actually using poor form or actually eating poor quality food. Interestingly, beneficial elements can also have a negative impact. For example, if the lifter has a genetic disposition that provides him with a leverage advantage in, let's say, The Snatch, he may develop poor habits or sub-optimal technique with his form. Or, maybe the lifter has exceptional overhead pushing strength and over time develops a loose catch, before sinking into the overhead squat. A loose catch will eventually limit their potential and can introduce injury, as they will always be trying to Press the Bar to the Bottom, rather than Ride the Bar to Bottom, during the overhead squat execution. Lifters constantly identify threats and eliminate vulnerabilities, as you can't train well, when you are injured. On the Money Management side, identifying Threats and Vulnerabilities is most critical. Most modern banking is done online, and it is wise to consider every part of the internet landscape as hostile territory.

Money Set

_____
_____
_____
_____
_____
_____
_____
_____
_____
_____
_____

Determine Risk Level

The ATV Matrix provides **Point-in-Time, On-Demand** modeling that changes as circumstances change. For example, if a Threat exists but the Vulnerability is neutralized, the overlap of the two corresponding circles is minimized. If the Vulnerability is not neutralized, the result is increased overlap, indicating higher Risk. A higher Asset value also increases Risk. The final level of Risk is then determined by the amount of **overlap** of all three elements.

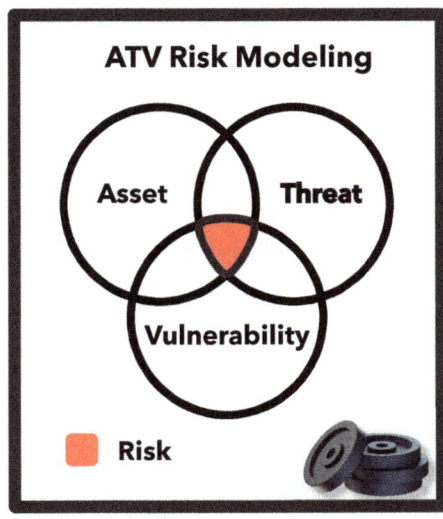

ATV Risk Modeling

Asset | Threat

Vulnerability

■ Risk

Analogue and Digital Basic Security Principles

The Master and Backup Repositories are the places where you will put all of the data associated with your Fisicality work. To reiterate, this is where ALL of your sensitive information will reside. It is critical that you secure these resources. Whether secured using analogue, digital, or a mix, there are specific guidelines that must be followed, to ensure data Confidentiality, Integrity, and Availability. Additionally, a cursory understanding of the Asset, Threat, Vulnerability Matrix will aid in implementing hardened security protocols. This is a broad area, and I am unable to cover it all here. It is up to you to conduct additional research on how best to harden your specific environment, for your resources.

Analogue Option

If you decide to go the analogue route, this can be something like a 3-ring binder, manila folder, brown paper bag, etc. There are also inexpensive pouches available online that provide a decent amount of protection from water and fire. And, this repository needs to be stored somewhere safe (like a safe — an actual safe) that is discreet, protected, secured, and durable.

Discreet
means it's not readily seen or easily accessed. The chances of accidental exposure is minimal.

Protected
means it's in a place that is resistant to environmental impacts. After all, a great hiding spot for your archive that is subject to water damage, if it gets wet, or is not resistant to warping, due to high but normal-range temperatures, is actually not that great of a hiding spot.

Secured
means that it has tamper resistance and hold-down power. It has a locking mechanism that challenges direct access, and it can't be quickly picked up and relocated.

Backup
all records at a secure, off site location, like a bank safety deposit box or private media vault. The backup should be synchronized frequently. A stale backup has low to no utility, as an authentication source.

Durable
means it can be accessed repeatedly without losing its integrity or ability to protect. This resource must be dependable, as access may be infrequent, but when you need it, it has to work as expected.

Digital Option

If you decide to go the digital route, encrypted hard drives, thumb drives, SSDs, and the like can all be found for reasonable prices. If you use a secure device, make sure you actually use the security features that it has and that you do so properly. For example, if you have an AES-256 encrypted drive and you set the password on it to

"mypassword123",

the device will not be hardened to attack like it would be if the password was

"mysuperduperPdDau~%~!iLZMA)b9ox$yZJ+Z]\hxzYv:@P/".

NIST Guidelines

According to NIST (National Institute of Standards and Technology) Special Publication 800-63B **(NIST, 2023)**, a few of their basic guidelines for a secure password include the items below. There are more, but these are the main ones. I have placed my thoughts, beside the ones I disagree with, in the HH sections.

Minimum 8 Characters.	No Consecutive Characters.	No Repeating Characters.
HH – Minimum 25 but Prefer 50 Characters.	**Examples:** • cdef • 4567 • !@#$	**Examples:** • mmmm • 4444 • ####

No Context or ID-Specific Words.	No Password Expiration.	No Special Characters.
Examples: • Job Title • Pet's Name • Car Model		**HH – Include Special Characters such as "#^%*$+!".**

Determine Tracking Mechanisms

It is important that you choose a tracking mechanism that will allow you the easiest path to maintain focus on your objectives. If you are spending an excessive amount of time trying to learn the intricacies of the tracking solution, rather than focusing on ferreting out what's happening with your actual finances, you may become discouraged or stop altogether. Of course, I believe the Hodgerian Fisicality Spreadsheet is the best solution, but I'm biased. Regardless of the tracking method you choose, please note that moving forward, I will use "Fisicality Worksheet" as a blanket term that encompasses all tracking methods. The initial solution does not need to be very sophisticated.

HANDWRITTEN LEDGER
This method provides the greatest connection to activity but requires relentless attention to detail.

 GOOD

ONLINE SOFTWARE
This method provides limited connection to activity, but can offer significant insight into trends and patterns.

 BETTER

COMPUTER SOFTWARE
This method provides an excellent balance between connection to activity, trends, customization, and efficiency.

 GREAT

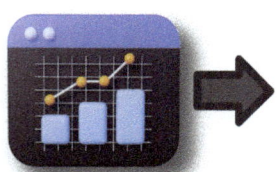

HODGERIAN FISICALITY
This method offers the highest level of connection to activity, customization, and flexibility but requires significant effort for initial deployment.

 ULTIMATE

SAMPLE MANUAL LEDGER

I used FTC Consumer website resources to create a modified version of the budget example below. This is a great online resource. Being a government site, I consider it an authoritative source for information. You can find the original version here:

https://consumer.gov/sites/default/files/pdf-1020-make-budget-worksheet_form.pdf

YEAR _____   MONTH _____

INCOME	Income Total
Paychecks (salary after taxes, benefits, and check cashing fees)	$
Other income (after taxes) for example: child support	$
Total Income	$

EXPENSES		Expense Total
HOUSING	Rent or mortgage	$
	Renter's insurance or homeowner's insurance	$
	Utilities (like electricity and gas)	$
	Internet, cable, and phones	$
	Other housing expenses (like property taxes)	$
FOOD	Groceries and household supplies	$
	Meals out	$
	Other food expenses	$
TRANSPORTATION	Public transportation and taxis	$
	Gas for car	$
	Parking and tolls	$
	Car maintenance (like oil changes)	$
	Car insurance	$
	Car loan	$
	Other transportation expenses	$
FAMILY/PERSONAL	Child care	$
	Child support	$
	Money given or sent to family	$
	Clothing and shoes	$
	Laundry	$
	Donations	$
	Entertainment (like movies and amusement parks)	$
	Health Care Expenses	$
FINANCE	Fees for cashier's checks and money transfers	$
	Prepaid cards and phone cards	$
	Bank or credit card fees	$
	Other fees	$
OTHER	School costs (like supplies, tuition, student loans)	$
	Other payments (like credit cards and savings)	$
	Other expenses this month	$
Total Expenses		$

$	—	$	=	$
Income		Expenses		Balance

The Anabolic Approach Explained

Track, Measure, & Adjust

You can't adjust something you're not measuring, and you can't measure something you're not tracking. When it comes to Money Matters, proper tracking of the correct elements can make what was once a hard decision a ridiculously easy one to make. Data driven trend lines often tell enlightening and compelling stories.

I recall hearing Dorian Yates discuss how he recorded every rep, set, and workout, for years. Though most bodybuilders may not go to this extreme and probably don't even use a dedicated log, they all still have some kind of way to measure progress. Powerlifters don't have the luxury for this kind of logging casualness.. Powerlifters are technicians. They record everything. They need precision to nail their percentages. This type of recording can provide insight into what needs to change, what needs to stay the same, and what behaviors precipitate desirable and undesirable outcomes. For an uninjured, consistently training, casual lifter who has recently hit a sticking point, or worse yet, discovered that they have plateaued in a particular area for several months (or even years), their tracking data can provide them with insight on what changes to make. Depending on the lifter and their circumstances, they may overestimate the positive and underestimate the negative or vice-versa. Similarly, in Money Matters, the investor may also overestimate the positive or negative, as well as underestimate them, depending on their circumstances.

Regardless of which phenomenon is at play, having well-captured historical data, readily available, can provide clarity and **neutralize inaccurate perceptions**. Now, I am a dinosaur and completely opposed to the proliferation of cell phone use for picture taking, video taking, and general intrusion, when it comes to working out. I'd go so far as to say that most people who regularly record their workout, or use a tripod with lights, or accost other lifters who are preventing them from "getting their shot" should be drop kicked through a goal post. However, even I concede that using the notes feature or an app to quickly log workout activity, is a good thing. Now, all you pesky kids, **GET OFF MY LAWN!**

Money Set

Track Your Money

For tracking and analyzing personal finance activity, the basic capability, low cost, advanced tooling, and interoperability of the **spreadsheet** is hard to beat.

FORCED REPS & DROP SETS

95%

Of Bodybuilders Perform

- **4-5 Exercises** per Muscle
- **3-6 Sets** per Exercise
- **7-9 Reps** per Set

(Alves et al., 2020)

FISICALITY

SECTION 3

TAKEOFF

Comprehensive Data Collection

When it comes to adept decision making, nothing is more important than the data. Poor judgement, ignorance, fear, and confusion can all be neutralized with access to clear, digestible, thorough data that are presented well.

Again, you can't gauge progress, if you don't measure. You can't measure what you don't track. You can't track what you haven't cataloged. And, you can't catalog what you haven't defined. This step begins with learning about what items are important to know about and then gathering information about those items. Then, where applicable, we will gather additional, periodic, point-in-time information about those same items. Using that information, we will make determinations about progress, as well as modification decisions on how best to proceed.

Feel free to over-capture data. As you engage in the process of managing your finances, you will find that the most relevant data has a way of elbowing its way to the front of the line for your attention. Most likely, you will end up creating tiered data resources, where the most used items are kept separately from the items you use less often. The basic items you will need to build the financial profile that details the current state of affairs for your fiscal health, includes but is not limited to:

- ▶ **Preliminary Razor**
- ▶ **Credit Report(s)**
- ▶ **Lexis Nexis Report(s)**
- ▶ **ChexSystems Report(s)**
- ▶ **Social Security Report**
- ▶ **Net Worth Report**
- ▶ **Paycheck Capture**
- ▶ **Accounts Database**
- ▶ **Razor Result**
- ▶ **Bank Statements**
- ▶ **Brokerage Statements**

All of this may be overwhelming at first, and that's OK. Unfamiliarity and uncertainty are to be expected at the start of any new endeavor. But, stick with it, put the work in, and eventually, you'll find the regular time commitment significantly reduced, while your mastery continues to steadily increase. Also, all of the initial data will become thinned out, as we begin to increasingly rely on only what we need for regular processing. Also, rarely used data will be pulled, as needed, from the archive but will not be included with the core, tactical dataset.

MORE ON MINDSET

> I know I'm going to be successful. I can see it clearly !

IMPORTANCE OF VISUALIZATION
Supercharge your learning by heavily utilizing images, videos, and visualization.

50% . . . of the human brain is required to process visual information.

78% . . . increase in learning and retaining info, by using visuals.

90% . . . of Information transmitted to the brain is visual data.

Thoughts and words have power. Your brain really doesn't distinguish fantasy from imaginings from reality very well. If you imagine yourself being successful, your brain reacts to the stimuli with many of the same responses as it would if it was happening in real life. Imagine yourself hitting a personal record in the bench press, or singing your favorite song to a standing ovation in the big show, or asking that cutie in your algebra class out and having her say, "Yes". Imagine every aspect of it, every detail – the scents in the air, the temperature, the light flickering through the leaves, the sequence of actions, and everything in between. Do the same with your fiscal planning and execution. Think of you managing your financial life. Imagine yourself with large balances in all of your core accounts.

Think of the peace of mind you feel being 100% debt free. Enjoy your unshakable confidence, reflecting on all of the knowledge you've gained. You are already that person. He already exists. You simply have to think it. Say it out loud. Write it down. Let that version of YOU reveal itself to this reality, by creating the proper environment and taking the proper actions to give him the best chance to succeed.

If you doubt the efficacy of what I'm saying, think of a time when you were done an injustice, belittled, or felt threatened, and you became angry or sad. Now, really put yourself back in that time and back at that place. Try to re-live the events as they happened, how they happened. Do this for 5 minutes, focusing on nothing but those unpleasant events. How do you feel? Is your heart racing? Is your posture stiffened? Is your mood darkened? Now, do this exercise again, but change the scenario to one where you experienced your greatest success. Was your response the same or different from the first result. Imagine if we choose (and it is a choice) to focus on thoughts where we develop intelligent plans, take action, overcome challenges, are successful in our endeavors, and fight to never give up. Winners think this way. What are you?

The Anabolic Approach Explained

The Power of Visualization

Weightlifters are obsessive about visualization, and most do it instinctively. They mentally perform lifts, run through routines, and complete entire workouts, over and over again, in their minds, and then do it some more. They imagine everything from chalking up and getting into position to determining how they plan to breathe on liftoff and controlling the negative. They also address everything before, in-between, and after each stage. Did I mention that they do this repeatedly, sometimes for days at a time? They put themselves in the action to the point that they can physically exhaust themselves by using the visualization exercises alone. Anyone watching would have just seen them sitting, somewhat detached but seemingly relaxed, while reclining in a chair.

Now this visualization super-power that weightlifters have developed can be extremely beneficial in other areas of their lives, if they choose it to be or if they are encouraged to use it. It is not uncommon to see a weightlifter excel in technical or engineering fields, because they will, for example, effectively be able to visualize completing the steps to deploy a server farm, or make perfect TIG-welded butt joints on their 1970 Chevelle, or walk through standing up the 1st floor framing, for their new family home.

These skills also transfer over to the white collar world, as the weightlifter will nearly always arrive to meetings prepared and be able to talk through the many complexities of whatever the current big project happens to be. I mean, after all, their psychic landscape has meticulously dissected every aspect of the project's execution so often that the mental walkthroughs that they thought were taking 10 minutes to complete were actually taking 2 hours. **Time passes differently** for them, when they are completely immersed and focused. Whether brushing their teeth, driving to work, typing a letter, troweling concrete, eating lunch, or watching the big game, the Anabolic athlete uses trivial moments to psychologically perfect their craft. This also means that when it comes to Money Matters, their visualizing the monthly bill paying cycle, investment cycle, or general Money Management activities results in reduced errors.

Money Set

_____

_____

_____

_____

_____

_____

_____

_____

_____

_____

_____

You Are a Story You Tell Yourself About You

According to science journalist, David McRaney, all of our memories are **confabulatory** constructs that are built On-Demand, and most of them are fictional. We recall myriad recorded snippets, from our brain's archives, and then assemble what we deem the memory. These **phenomenological qualia** are the reason why things like visiting a place you haven't been to in a while seems way different than how you "remember" it. This also means that immersive visualization can be just as powerful as "real" memories. **All we have to do is think It.**

(McRaney, 2011)

FORCED REPS & DROP SETS

Create the Preliminary Hodgerian Razor

The Hodgerian Razor is where we establish a real-world, uncomfortable to excruciatingly painful baseline. You should dread the idea of having to actually live the way The Razor would demand. If you experience significant discomfort with it, you'll know you did it right. This initial version is simply a way for us to begin bringing overlooked items, forgotten purchases, wasteful spending, recurring costs, and irrational assumptions to the fore. We don't want to actually spend a lot of time on this, as the final version is where we need to be 100% certain that we've captured everything. Once we have a manifest, it's time to start cutting.

The Initial Hodgerian Razor Matrix Template

What is a Philosophical Razor?

A philosophical razor is a guideline, principle, or intellectual system that seeks to remove, delete, or "shave off" anything associated with the subject, data, or phenomenon that is redundant, unnecessary, or superfluous. In other words, **it gets rid of all the stuff you might want but don't need.**

FAMOUS RAZORS

Occam's Razor
Explanations which require fewer unjustified assumptions are more likely to be correct; avoid unnecessary or improbable assumptions.

Hitchens' Razor
That which can be asserted without evidence can be dismissed without evidence.

Hanlon's Razor
Never attribute to malice that which can be adequately explained by stupidity.

(Meyer, n.d.)

WHO Do You Owe?	HOW Much Owed?
No Glow Electric & Power	$150
Mega Meats Grocery	$250
Academic Warning University	$2000
Jimmy No-Knees Loan Hut	$5,000
Principle First Mortgage Co.	$2,000

Step-by-Step: Creating the Initial Master List

1. Don't fret about duplicate entries, until you have completed adding data to the initial Razor's Master List.

2. Quickly write down everything you can remember purchasing over the last 30 days or so. Be attentive, but don't spend a lot of time on this initial step.

3. Review your merchant account portals, if you have them (Amazon, Wal-Mart, Target, Lowe's, etc.). Add their data.

4. Review and record your account activity for checking, savings, and CCs.

5. Now, identify and remove duplicate entries, and add what remains to your Razor Matrix. If there are any duplicates, I tend to keep the source of purchase entry. For example, if I have a purchase that shows up in my Amazon list and the credit card I payed with list, I'll remove the credit card entry from the Master List.

WHEN Is It Owed?	WHAT If It's Not Paid?	IS It Essential?	12-Month Razor Result?
Monthly	No Lights No Heat No Refrigeration	Yes	Pay
Bi-Monthly	No Food Go Hungry	Yes	Pay
Quarterly	Can't Matriculate Drop Out	No	Delay Pay
2 Months	Go On The Run OR Get New Kneecaps	Heck, Yeah!!!	Pay Or Else
Monthly	Loan Default Lose House	Yes	Pay

The Anabolic Approach Explained

It's Always Time for Some Action

Above all else, the Anabolic athlete is a man of action. He will do something. Even if he is ignorant of what needs to be done, he will still do something. Even if it's the wrong thing to do, he will still do that. And, then, he will make adjustments, based on the outcomes of those actions. Some people were fortunate enough to have had limited, personal instruction, minimal strength-focused PE class guidance, or participation in school sports to ease them into the strength training world. But, many didn't have that. Those folks typically ended up using books and magazines for guidance which sometimes resulted in complete beginners doing Advanced to Pro Level workout routines.

And then, there were those who just jumped right in, with no research at all. They knew that this thing called lifting weights existed, and it would give them big muscles and increased strength. So they found a workout spot and mimicked what they saw others doing, hoping they were doing it right. If they were lucky, they avoided injury, didn't blow all of their money on whatever the snake-oil supplement-of-the-day was, and maybe even were taken under the wing of and given direction by a more seasoned lifter, who subsequently gave them the sage wisdom to not do 5 lb. dumbbell curls in the squat rack. It's never OK to curl in the squat rack.

The bottom line here is the strength athlete will always take action and learn from their mistakes. The driven investor will also do the same. And, as with the strength athlete, hopefully they proceed cautiously enough to not endure much damage, due to being **overzealous and under-wise**; it's not uncommon to hear of inexperienced investors losing their retirement money or life's savings on risky stocks, cryptocurrency, or options trading. As always, **consider any losses as your tuition** to Low Loot University. People pay lots of money, to go to college and get degrees that oftentimes don't return much in the way of benefits or advantages. If you consider your first year of investing as school and the money you invest as tuition, cut the amount you think you need in half, and matriculate. The money spent is meaningless, as you can learn with a little, but the knowledge gained will be a lot.

Money Set

_____
_____
_____
_____
_____
_____
_____
_____
_____
_____
_____
_____

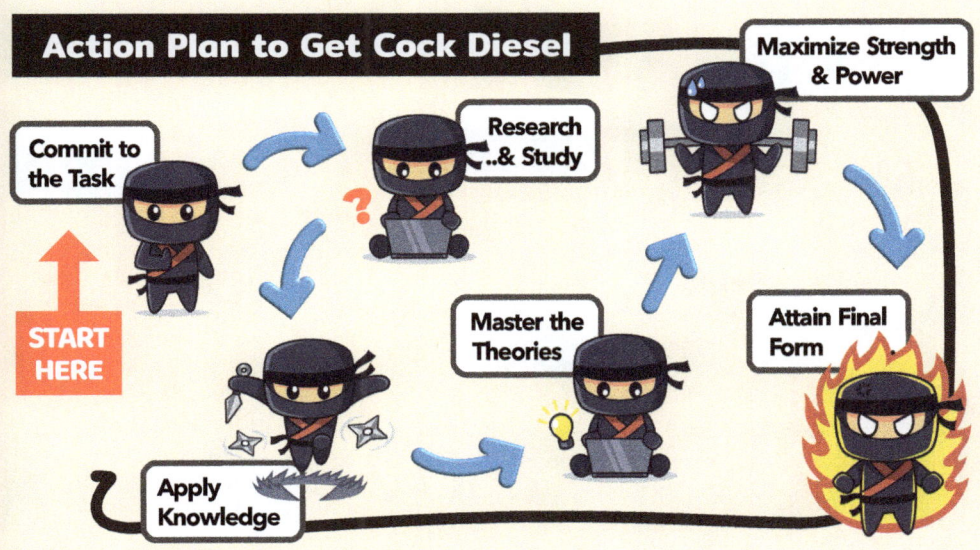

Obtain Your Credit Report

Free Credit Reports

The 3 main credit reporting bureaus are Experian, TransUnion, and Equifax. According to the Federal Trade Commission at https://www.ftc.gov/, you're entitled to 1 free copy of your credit report (but not FICO Score), every 12 months from each of the 3 nationwide credit reporting companies. You will need to provide your name, address, social security number, and date of birth to verify your identity. Call 1-877-322-8228, or order online from the only authorized website for free, here: https://www.annualcreditreport.com/.

Checking For Errors

Most negative information can remain on your credit report for up to 7 years, and bankruptcy information can remain for up to 10 years. However, if any information is incorrect, you can correct it via the dispute process. You can dispute in writing or online via web portal, for each of the 3 main bureaus. Once initiated, the credit bureaus have 30 days to complete their investigation.

How Is the FICO Score Calculated?
(myFICO, n.d.)

35% **PAYMENT HISTORY**
Late payments, collections, and bankruptcies lower this part of the score. As the largest factor in the scoring model, it has the most impact.

30% **AMOUNTS OWED**
This area reflects your credit utilization percentage. Ideally, this percentage should be 30% or less of your available credit.

15% **LENGTH OF CREDIT HISTORY**
This area reflects the average age of all of your credit accounts. Higher age values are scored more favorably than lower values.

10% **NEW CREDIT**
Hard inquiries are applications for new credit, and they negatively affect your score.

10% **CREDIT MIX**
Having several types of loans, such as installment (mortgage,auto, etc.) and revolving (credit card, and HELOCs), can raise your score.

3 Bureaus

According to the Fair Isaac Corporation, FICO Scores are calculated using weighted data grouped into the 5 categories, shown in the section to the left. These data are sourced exclusively from the 3 main credit bureaus.

715

Average U.S. Consumer Credit Score in 2024

FICO Scores

The Fair Isaac Corporation Score, or FICO Score, is a calculated value that uses data from the 3 main credit bureaus to determine a consumer's credit worthiness. Classic FICO scores range from 350 to 850. For the different scoring models, the exact formulas and criteria used to derive the score are unknown and are the subject of frequent criticism and controversy.

Disputes Contact Info

The U.S. Federal Trade Commission website has valuable information and resources about credit disputes, including links, videos, example letters, and much more. Go to:

https://www.ftc.gov/.

Credit Bureaus Direct

▶ **Equifax**
P.O. Box 740256
Atlanta, GA 30348
(866) 349-5191
https://www.equifax.com/

▶ **Experian**
P.O. Box 4500
Allen, TX 75013
(888) 397-3742
https://www.experian.com/

▶ **TransUnion LLC**
P.O. Box 2000
Chester, PA 19016
(800) 916-8800
https://www.transunion.com/

Tips to Improve Your Score

Your score can fall rapidly, but increasing it typically takes much longer. However, by fixing mistakes, paying down debt, and maintaining good history, significant progress can be made in 1 year or less.

▶ Dispute and Correct Errors
▶ Pay Bills on Time
▶ Reduce or Eliminate Debt
▶ Keep Unused Credit Cards Open
▶ Keep Credit Card Balances Low
▶ Negotiate to Remove Negative Info
▶ Avoid Going to Collections
▶ Don't Apply for Credit Too Often

Alternative Schedule

As you are eligible for 1 free credit report from each bureau annually, instead of getting all 3 at the same time, consider getting 1 report from a different bureau every 4 months. This will give you a better chance of catching mistakes and addressing issues.

FREE REPORT SCHEDULE

▶ **JAN - TransUnion**

▶ **MAY - Equifax**

▶ **SEP - Experian**

LexisNexis, ChexSystems, and Social Security Reports

LexisNexis

LexisNexis collects, aggregates, analyzes, and distributes consumer data, to its clients. Relevant business industries and sectors include insurance, legal, healthcare, government, and academic, to name a few. If you're giving blood, applying to college, getting a loan, applying for a job, or just found out your auto insurance company raised your rates, due to your driving habits that you DIDN'T report to them, it's probably LexisNexis providing the data. Get your free Consumer Disclosure Report and Description of Procedure Letter, from them, at: https://consumer.risk.lexisnexis.com/request.

ChexSystems Overview

Under the Fair and Accurate Credit Transaction Act (FACTA) amendments to the Federal Fair Credit Reporting Act (FCRA), you are entitled to request a free copy of your consumer report, once every 12 months. Additionally, ChexSystems also offers a free Consumer Score Report. This score is akin to the credit bureaus' FICO Score. ChexSystems retains reported information for 5 years. Call 1-800-428-9623, or order online from the only authorized website for free ChexSystems reports, here: https://www.chexsystems.com/.

ChexSystems Disclosure Report

Unlike your credit reports which track your transaction history for all visible accounts, the ChexSystems Report only captures negative information. This includes but is not limited to bounced checks, overdrafts, involuntary account closures, fraudulent activity, unpaid fees, etc., however you can dispute any errors. Sections of the report that return with a "No Information Found" status are desirable, for the consumer, and result in higher scores.

ChexSystems Consumer Score

This score ranges from 100 to 899, with a higher score being more favorable, as it indicates a lower risk. Different banks have different ChexSystems Score cutoff thresholds, but a score of 600 or greater would probably not get denied, unless there were other negative or unmet requirements. This score is one of several factors in the bank account approval process. Be assured, this system exists solely for the bank's benefit, not the consumer's.

Social Security Report

Generate a report on your lifetime recorded earnings with the Social Security Administration that shows the Work Year, Taxed Social Security Earnings, and Taxed Medicare Earnings. It can be found here: https://secure.ssa.gov/. A worker can earn 4 Work Credits each year and must earn 40, over their lifetime, to be eligible for benefits. Currently, in 2024, a worker earns 1 Work Credit for each $1,730 in wages. After qualifying, benefit projections for various start ages, can be found using the SSA Online Estimator. Typical milestone ages are:

Early Retirement - 62 • **Full Retirement - 67** • **Delayed Retirement - 70**

35 Years of Earnings To Compute Social Security Benefits

The SSA uses your highest 35 earning years to derive your **AIME** (Average Indexed Monthly Earnings). Then, it uses a formula to determine your monthly benefit, based on claiming the benefit at full retirement age, which is 67 for people born after 1959 (for some people born before 1960, this used to be age 66 and 6 months – that's one hell of a number). It uses all of this information to determine your **PIA** (Primary Insurance Amount) that's based on a sliding scale. Your final benefit is based on your age when you file.

Social Security Recipients By Age

🟩 All Recipients %   ⬛ All Adults %
(Scherer, 2023)

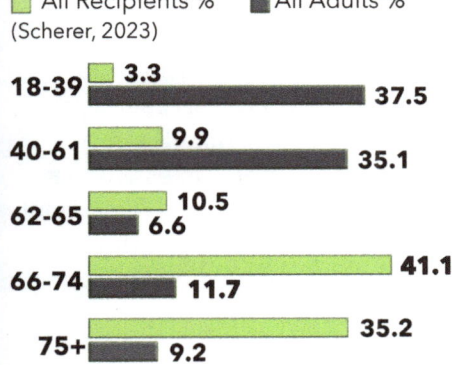

Age	All Recipients %	All Adults %
18-39	3.3	37.5
40-61	9.9	35.1
62-65	10.5	6.6
66-74	41.1	11.7
75+	35.2	9.2

Is Social Security About To Go Bankrupt?

No. Social Security is a Pay-As-You-Go system. It is funded through payroll taxes levied against the current workforce. Specifically, these taxes are: FICA (Federal Insurance Contributions Act) and SECA (Self-Employed Contributions Act) taxes. This myth started, because the Social Security Board of Trustees reported in 2021 that the Old-Age and Survivors Insurance and Disability Insurance (OASI and DI) Trust Funds will be depleted in 2033. These funds house surplus money, due to Social Security having received more than it payed out for several decades. It now pays out more than it receives, so these funds are being exhausted. Without resolution, benefits will be lowered, but not eliminated. The last time these funds experienced depletion risk was in 1983. The 98th Congress took action and raised payroll taxes, among other things, to resolve the concern.

(SSA Board of Trustees, 2021)

Net Worth Calculations

Your Net Worth is calculated by subtracting everything you owe from everything you have. Formally stated, it's the point-in-time balance of your Assets minus your Liabilities. It is not uncommon for people to have a negative Net Worth. In fact, a 2019 study by the Aspen Institute Financial Security Program reports 13 million American households, roughly 10.4% of the population, had a negative Net Worth (Nabi, 2022). Ways to improve Net Worth include:

▶ Decrease Your Liability Burden By Lowering Debt
▶ Increase Your Fixed and Liquid Asset Pool
▶ Improve and Increase the Market Value of Your Assets

Generate a report on your current Net Worth by subtracting all of your Liabilities from all of your Assets. To assist, you can use the Omni Net Worth Calculator, here: https://www.omnicalculator.com/.

Although money that you owe is a liability, I don't recommend money that is owed to you be classified as an asset. Theorectically speaking, money that is owed to you is your money, and you should be able to deploy it as a resource, but I recommend waiting until you take actual possession, before doing that. Also, I

don't include items that can't be readily sold or that have a targeted value that cannot be guaranteed. I mean, I like my 6 Million Dollar Man action figure, with the Roll-up Forearm Skin and Bionic Eye View-Hole in the skull, but nobody else values it at $10,000 like I do. And, even though you dropped a whole paycheck on it, selling that old fitness equipment that's masquerading as a clothes rack might only get you enough loot to buy a Micky D's double cheeseburger combo. Unless you can liquidate it reasonably quickly, it's fantasy money, in my opinion. It is important to be realistic when right-sizing input for this type of calculation. It is prudent to reduce or even eliminate any unreliable assumptions, when possible, and focus on concrete data. This will minimize issues associated with false narratives and overestimation, so any resultant miscalculations will be favorable.

ASSETS vs. LIABILITIES
(Leverage)   (Debt)

   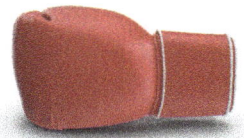

Sample Asset List   Sample Liability List

Savings Accounts   Credit Card Balances
Retirement Accounts   Consumer Debt
Real Estate   Mortgages
Vehicles   Primary Residence
Stock   Student Loans
Bonds   Vehicle Loans
Certificates of Deposit   Primary Vehicle
Cryptocurrency   Borrowed Cash

DEFINITIONS   If uncertainties arise when attempting to classify an item as an asset or liability, consider the flow of money for the item. Assets cause money to flow towards you, and Liabilities cause money to flow away from you.

REAL ESTATE   If you own property that you rent out, that's an asset. However, the property that acts as your residence is a liability. A property that you live in and also rent out a portion of has percentage-based characteristics of both an asset and a liability.

VEHICLES   Similar to real estate, vehicles that are exclusively for your use are liabilities. However, vehicles that have some portion of their use dedicated to generating cash flow are assets by that proportion.

RECEIVABLES   Money that is owed to you that you expect to receive within one year can be classified as an asset. However, I recommend caution, here. Personally, I disregard most receivables for my practical use Net Worth Calculation.

TRACKING   Net Worth Tracking is built into the Fisicality spreadsheet, and it should be updated monthly. If your Net Worth is currently negative, it is a significant milestone to break through top-soil and get above ground. With consistent effort, you can do it!

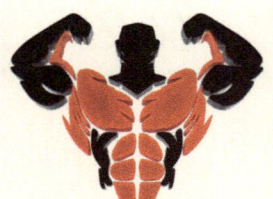

The Anabolic Approach Explained

Never Abandon the Basics

The Anabolic athlete demands results, doesn't like to waste resources, is always scanning for something new that can aid progress, and constantly seeks to eliminate existing elements that hinder progress. They are always asking themselves questions. Is this a good exercise for this muscle? Does this supplement work? Should I switch my training time around? Should I use free weights or machines, for this body part? What's the best gear to use? The questions come non-stop. And, then they repeat, over and over. The supplement industry takes advantage of this behavior by constantly introducing new supplements, updated formulas, enhanced versions, and special products that are often times ineffective or worse yet, harmful. It's important for the lifter to know when a supplement, exercise, piece of equipment, training approach, or any other thing is an asset or a liability. Occasionally, it may take some time to figure this out, but as soon as he knows, he must make the change, rather than continuing, as before.

The bottom line here is, just like in the Money Management world, if you find something is an asset, **Keep It or Acquire It**; if you find something is a liability, **Discard It or Avoid It**. The caveat here is that some things can be one or the other, depending on your purpose for using it or the timing of when you need to use it. The bodybuilder may find that excessive jump rope work is a liability, when they are trying to bulk up, but also find that it's a perfect exercise to increase fat burning when cutting down. Similarly, the investor may find that automatically investing the paid dividends is too limiting and a liability, when they are aggressively trying to grow their portfolio balances, but they may conversely find it's perfect for set-it-and-forget-it investing, once their portfolio has matured.

Ultimately, whether discussing weight training or financial matters, it is critical to not confuse essential, core elements with supplemental add-ons. Excessive trading in speculative securities will not replace or outperform simple investing in solid, blue chip companies; and consuming powdered shakes and proprietary drinks will not replace the quality and effectiveness of eating real food.

Money Set

_____

_____

_____

_____

_____

_____

_____

_____

_____

_____

_____

_____

INCLINE PRESS

BARBELL SQUAT

BARBELL ROW

If I Could Only Choose 3 Lifts

Choosing the most effective tools and methods, for your stated goals, can be simplified by restricting your options to only the most essential elements. From a lifting perspective, I would choose multi-joint exercises that allow me to move my heaviest weights. Here, I opt for a barbell row over the deadlift, after much angst and gnashing of teeth.

Create Paycheck and Account Capture Databases

Having detailed, core data about your paycheck, as well as all of your accounts is invaluable. When updating records, paying bills, verifying status, calling in to vendor support, or resolving an issue with a creditor, you will have all of the necessary information at your fingertips. Knowing that you can quickly retrieve account data when needed will lower anxiety, improve accuracy, increase efficiency, and optimize interactions with vendors.

For your paycheck database, include all information in distinct columns. This simple spreadsheet will allow you to track your inflows, as well as alert you to any inaccuracies, changes, or anomalies. And, it will also provide you with a historical record that allows you to quickly retrieve data associated with a milestone or event. For the Account Databases, the more detail provided the better. Here, you want to think through scenarios to help you get ideas about what data to capture. Think about what you will need, if there is a problem, a warranty issue, an interaction with support, a termination of services, etc. Having information related to these things will help you with items, such as speeding up getting to the correct support resource, or ensuring you have the right PIN Code for privileged access, or ensuring you don't get hit with a cancellation fee, because you didn't have the correct info to properly initiate a cancellation.

Not All States Require Pay Stubs

(Paystub, n.d.)

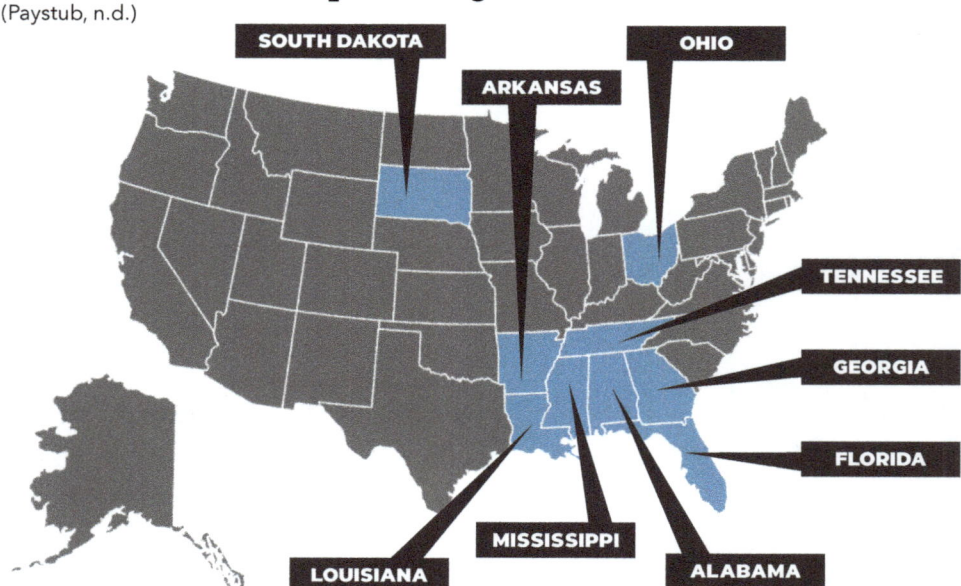

The states above do not require employers to provide pay data to employees. The federal Fair Labor Standards Act requires employers to record and retain payroll records but does not require them to provide this information to employees. If you find yourself in a situation where you aren't provided pay data, you will need to submit a records request with the employer. This data generally includes the pay period start and end dates, gross wages, taxes, deductions, employer contributions, and net pay.

A Database is Just a Glorified Spreadsheet

OK, I'm being more than a little bit facetious here. The most basic, properly structured database can handle infinitely more data, much more gracefully, than the most robust spreadsheet. However, for our purposes, the spreadsheet offers more than enough functionality for us to achieve all of our management, administration, and tracking goals. But, for those of you with the technical chops to do it, or for those of you who simply want to learn database management, graduating to deploying one can be an interesting project. One of the main benefits you will realize by starting with the spreadsheet first is that you will be very knowledgeable about your financial data and have a mental model of what it looks like when designing your database structure. As a final word, though, I have never found a need to migrate pass the spreadsheet.

ACCOUNT DATA ADMINISTRATION

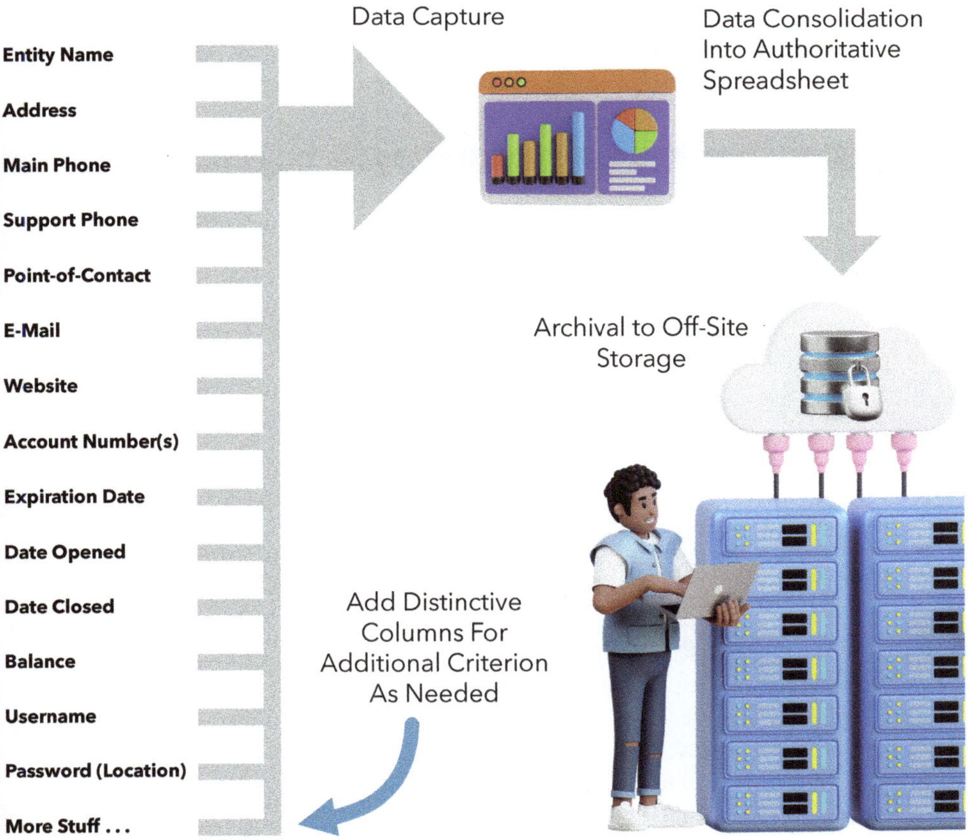

Data Capture

Data Consolidation
Into Authoritative
Spreadsheet

Entity Name

Address

Main Phone

Support Phone

Point-of-Contact

E-Mail

Website

Archival to Off-Site
Storage

Account Number(s)

Expiration Date

Date Opened

Date Closed

Add Distinctive
Columns For
Additional Criterion
As Needed

Balance

Username

Password (Location)

More Stuff . . .

Generate the Final Razor Result

Using the Initial Razor Result you completed earlier, generate the final report on your current absolute minimum money required to live with zero luxuries, zero extras, zero non-essentials, zero comforts, or zero peripherals. This is one of the hardest parts of the whole program, identifying waste and the items you will be giving up. If you're like me, you'll find that you spend a lot more money than you think on certain things. I recall at one point, I was spending several hundred dollars a month eating out, in addition to what I was consuming at home. Controlling the impact of your consumption triggers and maintaining discipline on how you respond to them is non-negotiable.

$15 BILLION
U.S. Credit Card Late Fees
(CFPB, 2023)

ANNUALLY

Credit Card spending is deceptive. It is habitual and easily overlooked. Only by tracking it do you get an idea of its, oftentimes negative, impact on your finances. As the average credit card interest rate is ~**23%** and monthly interest payment is ~**$125**, this is one area to monitor closely.

WHO Do You Owe?	HOW Much Do You Owe?	WHEN Do You Owe It?
Hometown Power Co.	126	Monthly
Hometown Water Co.	57	Monthly
Vroom Vroom Auto	400	Monthly
Dropouts Student Loans	500	Monthly
Paradise Estates Rent	1200	Monthly
We Keeps It Storage	100	Monthly
Jimmy No-Knees & Assoc.	5000	2 Months
Super Speedy Internet	80	Monthly
Connectrix Cellular	90	Quarterly
Mehcks Movies and Things	200	Annually
Bigflix Movies and Things	15	Monthly
Dismal Movies and Things	15	Monthly
Grocery Foodery	610	Monthly
Ghouls Gym	400	Annually
Mower Maniacs Lawn Co.	80	Monthly
Gambling Emporium	400	Monthly
Burger Boy Fast Food	120	Monthly

ACTUAL MONEY

We won't be using too many fancy terms, but some are necessary. Regardless of the source or the destination, we will focus on referring to things, based on how they are used in the real world. **Revenue** is income earned from selling things. **Profit** is what you have left over, after subtracting how much it cost you to produce the thing you sold from how much you sold it for. **Cash Flow** shows the exact amount of money, with no trickery, that's flowing in and flowing out. Businesses use a lot of intricate language with nuanced interpretations. The same amount of actual money can be reported and interpreted differently, depending on how a company is structured and how many reporting gymnastics are at play. We won't do any of that. Instead, we will plainly record non-distorted, non-manipulated, point-in-time Net Cash Flow.

GROSS CASH FLOW
The sum of all successful transactions for incoming money only.

NET CASH FLOW
The sum of all successful transactions for incoming money, minus all outgoing money.

WHAT Happens If You Don't Pay?	IS It Essential For Survival?	12-MONTH Razor Result
No Electricity	Yes	Keep
No Water	Yea	Keep
Fees, Car Repossessed	No	Keep
Fees, Wage Garnishment	No	Keep
Kicked Out	Yes	Keep
Lose Items to Auction	No	Discard
Bodily Harm, Property Damage	Yes	Keep
Service Disabled, No Internet	No	Keep
No Cellular Service	No	Keep
Entertainment Reduced	No	Discard
Entertainment Reduced	No	Discard
Entertainment Reduced	No	Discard
No Food, Don't Eat	Yes	Keep
Lose Gym Access	No	Keep
Grass Not Cut, Must Buy Mower	No	Discard
Addiction Withdrawal	No	Discard
Guilty Pleasure Gone	No	Discard

FISICALITY

SECTION 4

Define and Refine the Money Matrix

Defining the Money Matrix Structure is a fancy way of saying which accounts you are going to create. **Refining** the Money Matrix is determining which of the created accounts you are going to actively use, for specific purposes, at specific stages of your plan. This is the modeling aspect. Personally, I like creating separate accounts for each bucket of money, but this may not be an option, if your bank restricts the number of accounts you can create. However, keep in mind that online banking has made opening multiple accounts extremely easy to do. Also, many banks now allow you to create separate buckets within a single account, somewhat eliminating the need for multiples. Even so, I still like the separate accounts, as I find the hard, segregated structure simpler and more trustworthy. I don't have to worry about cross contamination, as I do if there is a problem with an inter-account bucket.

And, if a segregated account is compromised, I don't have to necessarily worry about it affecting my other accounts, by default. Ultimately, each person has to determine what works best for them, and it is perfectly acceptable and expected that, starting off, you will have a simpler structure. I have included examples below for Minimalist, Standard, and Extreme models. Aside from that, my personal approach and recommendation here is that you account for every penny of your money— **and I mean EVERY SINGLE PENNY – and then make sure that each one is doing EXACTLY what you want it to do.**

MINIMALIST **The Minimalist Structure is for someone who wants a simplified model that has fewer accounts and someone who is also comfortable with more complex tracking requirements. At a minimum, this structure consists of 1 Checking and 1 Savings account that are both actively being leveraged. Tracking via ledger is crucial for this account.**

OPTIMAL **The Optimal Structure is what someone who desires more account isolation than the Minimalist Structure provides, as well as the benefit of more simplified tracking. Here, we start to utilize separate accounts for paying bills, managing projects, isolating frivolous funds, and building an emergency fund.**

EXTREME **In the next section, we will review the Extreme Fund in detail. Only a cursory overview of the Minimalist and Optimal funds were given above, as the functions and separation used by those accounts can be synthesized from the Extreme Model. Simply take what's needed from the Extreme, and deploy for any of the others.**

Account Progression

Use a mock Occam's Razor, and only create the accounts that are needed for comfort and no more.

CURRENT STATE

1 Functional Account

Here, there may be 2 accounts in reality, a checking and a saving. But, if no money is actually being saved, then in essence, it's just 1 account.

MINIMALIST

2 - 4 Functional Accounts
Checking and Savings are separated, and money is starting to be organized, based on function.

OPTIMAL

4 - 8 Functional Accounts

Accounts are organized into a well defined, purposeful structure. Activity tracking is simplified, and management efficiency is enhanced.

EXTREME TRANSITION

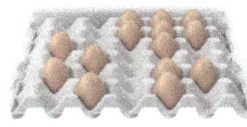

Create as many accounts as needed, for what your plan is. Each distinct, granular purpose is given its own resource account. The structures are created, but not all of the accounts are fully funded or utilized.

EXTREME

Create as many accounts, as needed. All initiatives and purposes have accounts that are distinct, fully-funded, connected, and actively being used. This structure scales to effectively administer complex account architectures and interrelationships.

> **THE BEST TYPE OF LOAN, IS THE ONE YOU DON'T MAKE; BETTER THAN THAT, IS THE ONE YOU DON'T TAKE.**
>
> —CHARLES HODGE

The Hodgerian Extreme Model

Each account section has a distinct purpose. The **Operations Box** accounts are used to facilitate money ingress and primary distribution (Moving Loot). The **Battle Box** accounts provide core and extended security (Keeps Me Safe). **The Vault** extends capability and adds broad-spectrum assets (Leveling Up). The **Builder Box** facilitates increased diversification and new technology research (Exploration). Excluding All Debt Payoff, you can easily gauge the maturity of your Money Management, based on where most of your activity takes place.

Beginner Level activity is focused primarily in the Operations Box. This is where a person is mostly paying bills and funneling money into the Plans account, because they are planning on moving, getting a car, preparing for a new roof, etc. This is the most basic category, and its activity can easily be handled with 1 or 2 accounts. **Novice** Level activity is focused primarily in the Battle Box. This is the category where countermeasures for emergency and hardship scenarios are stored. All accounts that we work with are worked simultaneously. The defining factor is the percentage of resources each account is granted at any given time, based on its level of focus. To further clarify, I may be putting money into all of these accounts, but if building the ICS account is the focus, it's going to get the largest percentage of money within the Battle Box group. And, if we go up a level, the same logic applies. Hence, if The Battle Box is the area of focus, at a particular time, it's going to receive the largest percentage of money that's allocated to the collective 4 main groups.

Intermediate Level activity is focused primarily within The Vault. If you find that the largest percentage of your time, research, money, and management activity is taken up by Vault activity, you are comfortably at the Intermediate level. **Advanced** activity takes place primarily in the Builder Box. The Builder Box is similar to The Vault, except it is not tax advantaged but instead enjoys flexibility and freedom of movement that The Vault accounts lack. One of the keys to success is to recognize when focus needs to shift between groups. Vault activity is far and away the most pleasurable and intellectually satisfying category for me to spend most of my time. I also enjoy watching Battle Box balances grow, as well as some of the activity in Plans (getting a new car, for example). But, none of those things come close to the level of engagement and satisfaction I get with Vault activity. I think it has something to do with the Vault money being somewhat of an untouchable, delayed gratification which makes decisions for it seem more grave. Builder Box activity is used as somewhat of a test bed for Vault decisions.

So, how many accounts does an Extreme structure have? Well, as I've said before, you can have as many as you need to have, depending on your circumstances, activity, financial vehicles, and management thesis. The example on the next page is how my current structure is setup. I have 65 distinct accounts active, of which 52 are CD accounts. The Builder Box funds practically exist in one account, even though they are logically segregated in my spreadsheet. If I had more money, say a few hundred thousand dollars dedicated to distribute to each category, I would set them up into their own dedicated accounts. But, as it stands now, they all gracefully exist within the same account.

STRUCTURE TREES

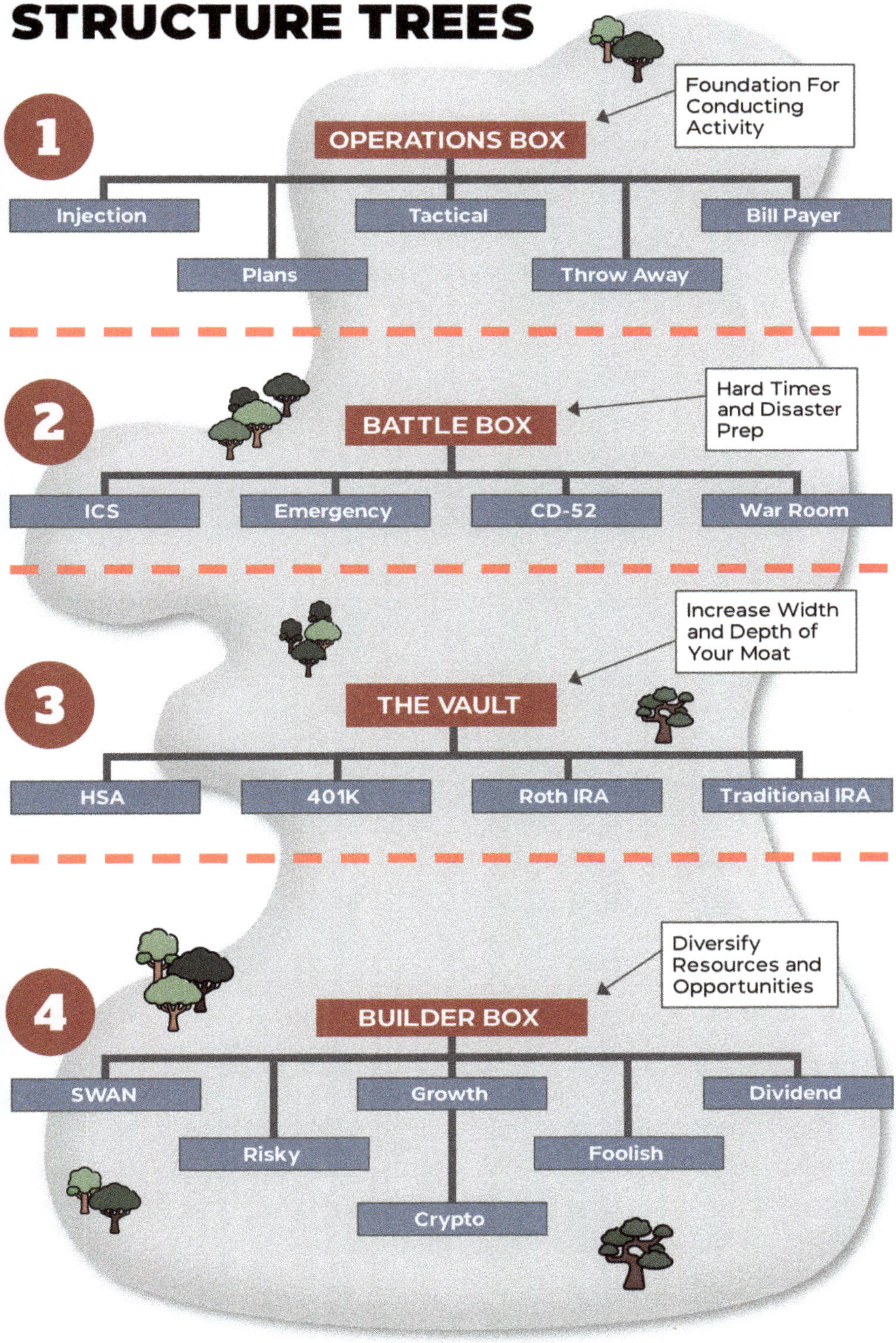

1 OPERATIONS BOX

Foundation For Conducting Activity

- Injection
- Plans
- Tactical
- Throw Away
- Bill Payer

2 BATTLE BOX

Hard Times and Disaster Prep

- ICS
- Emergency
- CD-52
- War Room

3 THE VAULT

Increase Width and Depth of Your Moat

- HSA
- 401K
- Roth IRA
- Traditional IRA

4 BUILDER BOX

Diversify Resources and Opportunities

- SWAN
- Risky
- Growth
- Crypto
- Foolish
- Dividend

The Anabolic Approach Explained

Take Your Time and Choose Wisely

Choosing the correct workout is essential for success for the strength athlete. The workout plan must align with the lifter's goals, experience level, and capabilities. For example, an experienced lifter who hasn't touched a weight in 5 years should probably not try to start off using the same Advanced workout that they were using, prior to them stopping 5 years earlier. They may not need to start with a Beginner routine, but a Novice routine should be more than enough. Similarly, the elite long distance runner, who has never touched a weight, should probably start with a Novice routine. Even though they are an experienced athlete with amazing capabilities in their sport, they are **attempting something new** that will stress their muscles, tendons, ligaments, nervous system, and joints very differently. The surface exertion will seem very familiar, during the workout, but the impact in the days post workout will be debilitating, if they attempt an Intermediate or Advanced workout.

The most important thing for beginners (and experienced lifters who have been away) is to work on learning and using the correct form, cadence, load, and frequency, for working out safely and effectively. They must also not place that which is **desired but not needed** before that which is **needed but not desired**. This would be things like using supplements, rather than eating real food, or using accessory exercises, like double inverted, reverse tricep kick backs and assisted negative, oblique side bends, rather than heavy, core compound lifts like squats and presses.

The idea starting out is to focus on gaining experience and using proper form, with modest weight to minimize complications, while maximizing development. A 65 lb. bench press can easily turn into a 405 lb. bench press, after a few years of dedicated training. You'll be happy you mastered the basics, when it does. For the investor, the same techniques apply. Learn the basics with modest amounts of money, before using large sums. Starting off with risky, advanced, options trading techniques, before investing a meager amount of money into an S&P 500 Index Fund, will most likely end in disaster. So, start slow, and make thoughtful decisions.

Money Set

_____
_____
_____
_____
_____
_____
_____
_____
_____
_____
_____
_____

Most Popular Exercises
(Richter, 2023)

1. Bench Press – 25.36%
2. Squat – 15.88%
3. Deadlift – 11.37%
4. Lat Pulldown – 8.53%
5. Overhead Press – 8.29%
6. Barbell Row – 7.58%
7. Dumbbell Lateral Raise – 6.64%
8. Leg Extension –5.69%
9. Barbell Curl – 5.69%
10. Tricep Pushdown – 4.98%

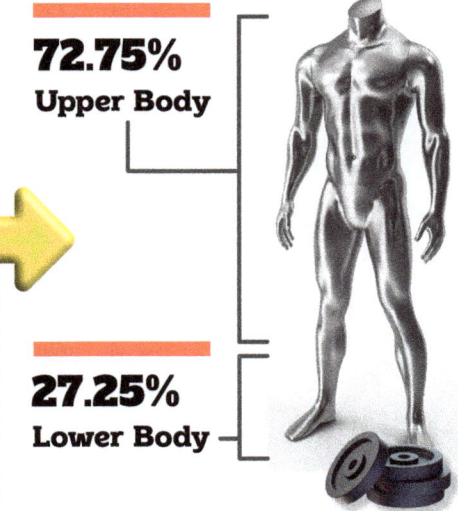

72.75%
Upper Body

27.25%
Lower Body

Operations Box

Operations, in a business sense, involves organizing, planning, and supervising to deliver a desired outcome for defined goals. Because this group of 5 accounts also contains the only 3 that administratively allow ingress and egress of external money, I consider it operationally functional. Additionally, Bill Payer is uniquely interesting to the Fisicality Worksheet, due to its intended purpose.

INJECTION

Injection is fed by external sources, and its only purpose is to act as an ingress point, by having all incoming money routed to it. It does not have checks, a debit card, or a credit card associated with it. Money sent to this account is meant to be immediately routed to either Bill Payer or Plans for further processing.

TACTICAL

Tactical is incidental money that can be withdrawn from a teller machine. It is designed to have $300 in it, for minimal risk of loss. It is the only managed account that has a Bank/Debit/CC associated with it.

PLANS

Plans are target based buckets for specific projects, acquisitions, or engagements. This includes moving expenses, car down payments, house down payments, new furniture, vacations, wardrobe updates, new swimming pool, etc. Plans also acts as a holding tank, until Bill Payer is ready to process.

THROW AWAY

Throw Away money is exactly what its name suggests. This is money that you can blow on impulse purchases, give to the hobo holding a sign, or throw out of the window of a skyscraper, to watch folks' reactions below.

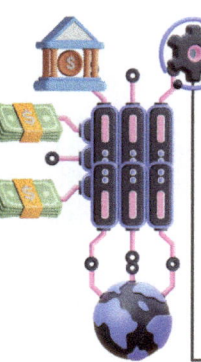

BILL PAYER

Bill Payer can be fed by any account and is meant to be the primary distribution hub for all external money outflows. Monthly bills, scheduled payments, expected distributions, and planned transfers are routed through and satisfied via this account. For example, if a transfer from the IRA account to the brokerage account is needed, it flows through this account.

How These Accounts Work Together

All inbound money is deposited into Injection before immediately being routed to Bill Payer for processing, which I believe enhances security. It offers a smaller ingress footprint and also provides isolation, so that if I see money being sent from that account (or any account that's not Bill Payer, for that matter) to an outside source, I'll know something is wrong. The important thing to note is that, as a rule, all money eventually traverses the Bill Payer account. In most cases, money in Injection and Bill Payer rarely sits for more than a few hours. I've already planned what to do with the money, so there is no reason for it to sit. Although accounts such as

Tactical, Plans, and Throw Away are internal accounts, they are still administered as line items in the Fisicality Worksheet; they are essentially treated like any other bill. This keeps things very simple, as it removes any special circumstances or anomalies.

Rules Don't Mean Anything, If You Don't Follow Them.

So, we've spent the time to create a system that has clear protocols. All we have to do now is follow it. By every account being treated in the exact same manner, errors, oversights, and miscalculations are reduced. You also won't waste energy trying to recall that special situation, for that one time, when you did that different thing, from over a year ago. The simplified Fisicality flow is:

Money ➡ **Injection** ➡ **Plans (Holding Area for Bill Payer)** ➡ **Bill Payer** ➡ **Any Internal or External Account**

All Debt Payoff

All Debt Payoff contains larger debt items, such as mortgages, car notes, CC balances, etc., but it can contain debts of any size. The list is pulled from items already in the Fisicality Worksheet or your ledger, depending on the tracking method you chose (as a reminder, I am using "Fisicality Worksheet" to refer to any tracking method, including ledgers and apps). Reducing or completely paying off debt is arguably the single most important aspect and goal of personal finance. Sure, having funds set aside in case of an emergency is important and so is socking away money for retirement. However, I can think of no other thing that's as impactful for regular folks as eliminating debt. Having low to no debt empowers a person by allowing them to divert significantly more funds to projects, retirement, vacations, investments, and any other thing that strikes a fancy.

28%
Guaranteed Return on Your Money

According to Forbes Advisor, for July 30, 2024, the average credit card APR in the U.S. was 27.62%. The historical average investment return for the S&P 500 is 10.51% (with dividends reinvested). To get a guaranteed return of 28%, the average person simply has to pay off their credit cards.   (Black, 2024)

AVERAGE DEBT

Average household debt in the U.S. across mortgages, auto loans, student loans, and credit cards is
$104,215
(Horymski, 2024)

THE NET WORTH METRIC
When attempting to eliminate debt, instead of focusing on the balance of the individual accounts, use Net Worth as your guiding metric. Adopting this approach will ensure that you maintain the proper mindset, to make the best decisions, on your way to achieving your goals. With this method, it makes sense to prioritize eliminating credit card debt, rather than speculative investing. And, did I mention it's also a guaranteed return?

Regardless of how much money a person has coming in each month, their situation is better, if they have no debt. The best way to control debt is to not acquire it in the first place. But, we all have made mistakes with those 8 compact discs for 1¢ from Columbia House Music, the rent-to-own radio, or smorgasbord from the comic book ads consisting of the Spud Gun, Sea Monkeys, Whoopee Cushion, Finger Snapping Gum Pack, and 8-in-1 Super Tool. Or, later in college, maybe it was the no questions asked credit cards or the used car that you'd figure out how to pay for, as each monthly note came due. When you start off, you may need to split initiatives into multiple cycles to achieve all of your goals, via Cycle 1 (first half of the month) and Cycle 2 (second half of the month). After paying it off, the hundreds of dollars that used to go towards interest on credit cards can be used for projects, plans, and investments. Having a larger chunk of money to work with allows you to prepare and execute better. For most people, unless they are already debt free, I suggest All Debt Payoff be their primary Objective.

STAY ABOVE $0

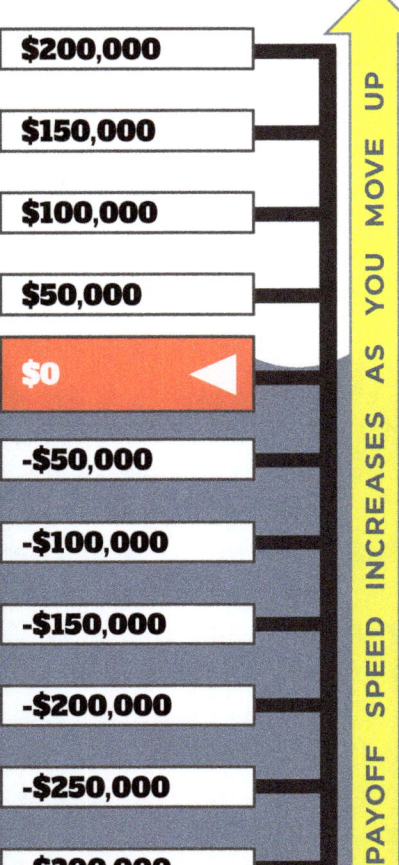

$200,000

$150,000

$100,000

$50,000

$0 ◀

-$50,000

-$100,000

-$150,000

-$200,000

-$250,000

-$300,000

PAYOFF SPEED INCREASES AS YOU MOVE UP

ADP's Bifurcated Entries
▶ **Entry 1:** The agreed to minimum obligation entries that are tracked and payed, as part of the regular monthly payment in the Operations Box, using **Razor Result Funds**.
▶ **Entry 2:** The aggressive pay down of ADP, using **After Shave Funds**.

NEGATIVE NET WORTH HOUSEHOLDS
▶ **Are 14% Of U.S. Households**
▶ **45% Is Automobile Debt**
▶ **Home Holds 20% Of Wealth**
▶ **Has 36% Of Mortgages Underwater**

POSITIVE NET WORTH HOUSEHOLDS
▶ **15% Is Automobile Debt**
▶ **Home Holds 40% Of Wealth**
▶ **Has 4% Of Mortgages Underwater**

(Desjardins, 2016)

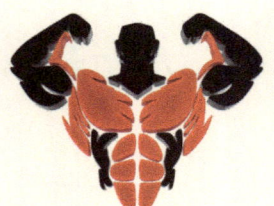

The Anabolic Approach Explained

Fiscal and Physical Net Worth

If the anabolic athlete takes inventory of all of their actions, behaviors, and abilities, would they consider their subjective balance to be positive or negative. Things such as smoking, drug use, alcohol use, insufficient sleep, poor nutrition, wasting money, and negative interpersonal interactions are all things that, directly or indirectly, reduce their Fiscal and Physical Net Worth. Things such as being lifetime injury free, metabolically healthy, well rested, and nutritionally responsible are all things that increase their Physical Net Worth. Most things affecting Physical Net Worth are behaviorally influenced. Things such as genetics or environmental factors are not behavioral, however they can be leveraged or enhanced, based on behavior. The idea here, for the lifter, is to increase their Physical Net Worth, over time. Unlike Financial Net Worth which has theoretically limitless potential, Physical Net Worth is capped. You will get to a point where you can no longer add weight to the bar, increase reps, raise your work capacity, add more muscle, etc. On the fiscal side, however, there will always be something else to diversify into, invest in, or generate a return on. The opportunities may diminish, but you can always do more. On the physical side, whether they know it or not, **everyone wants to be a bodybuilder**.

As years lengthen into decades, increasing and maintaining ability is the true reward. Over time, the main criterion must shift focus from **Quantitative** Output to **Qualitative** Ability. As you get older, being able to perform and excel outside of your age range becomes the standard. If you are able to functionally perform the way someone years to decades younger can, your Physical Net Worth (and subsequent quality of life) is considered high. Science and technology have provided things to aid us with this, such as hormone therapy, advanced surgical repair procedures, science-based nutrition, and optimized workout routines. Just as it pays financially to start investing early, due to the phenomenon of compounding, it also pays physically to start training early, to benefit from adding as much quality muscle as you can, while your biochemistry is optimized to do so. Even without sarcopenia, age-related muscle loss accelerates after age 80.

Money $et

70-Year-Old, Lifelong Exercisers Are 40 Years Younger Physiologically

- Based on Skeletal Capillarization &
- Metabolic Enzymes

(Gries et al., 2018)

Battle Box

A warrior prepares for War during Peace time. If War is thrust upon you, and you only begin preparing for it – under duress, under fire, and under attack – after its already started, you're too late. You are now in a situation where you need to determine how much damage you are willing to take and where you are willing to take it, in order to preserve what you deem to be most important. For example, on the few occasions I've had spiky objects directed towards me by folks who were sincerely intent on using them, I had to make a conscious choice on what body part to sacrifice, in order to neutralize the threat. Typically, this has always been the backs of my arms. And, if I had a shirt or some other cloth to quickly wrap around that sacrificial limb, that was good for me. But, again, in these types of situations, there is no reasoning, there is no escape, something is going to go down, and the question you face is, "What are you going to do"? Doing nothing is not always an option. **Sometimes, you getting dealt with is unavoidable. And, savages don't care about how tough you THINK you are, how big your muscles are, your reputation, or the potential danger you pose. In the jungle, the rule is, "Let's Find Out". Sed, I wuz.**

It's easy to say what you would do in a situation when watching an event or movie, in the comfort of your own home, sitting on the couch, with a cold drink in your hand. But, what about when you're in a strange town, in a strange place, among people that mean to do you harm – and you're all ALONE? The exit is blocked. All you have to rely on is yourself. No one else is coming to save you. And, **if you can't do it, it will not get done.** I've been in this type of situation several times. It is NOT fun. Additionally, I'm a loner by nature, so aside from the luxury afforded me back when I was with my rock-solid college dawgs, I've rarely had much in the way of a crew, squad, or group to back me up. If anything, during most of the times I was with people who I thought I could depend on, I was left dangling, alone in the wind – except for a very few occasions with the very few, truly hardcore; I talked about some of them at the beginning of this book.

I say all of this, so that you who can relate, you'll understand that you need to have that same, Battle Ready mentality to prepare your War Room for Bad Times. In a grid down situation, you'll need resources: food, shelter, water, clothing, protections, communications, money, and supplies, to outlast the Bad Thing. You'll also need all of those same things, if you lose your job. And, for those of you who haven't yet endured Bad Times, where you only had yourself to rely on, you need to imagine and artificially put yourself in that place. From a **confabulatory** perspective, it won't matter. You want to go into battle with fully formed calluses and sufficient scar tissue, even if it's only from training, role-playing, or visualization. Yes, you prepare for War during Peace time.

ICS

In Case Stuff happens fund. I've had people tell me that I use a different word for the "S", but I can assure you that it has always been "stuff", and that's all I have to say about that. This fund is for exigent circumstances that are unexpected, and they must be addressed immediately.

EMERGENCY

The Emergency account was built primarily as a 3-6 month survivability fund. However, it can be directed to any other fiscal emergency, as needed. Months 4, 5, and 6 of this account were added as a cushion, as realistically, if you have something going on for more than 3 months, it's not an emergency anymore; after 3 months, what was an emergency is now just normal life for you. And, normal can be planned for. It may have started as an emergency, but it would be a mistake to classify it as such, after 3 months. Reevaluate and reclassify, as necessary, any emergency situation, after 3 months.

CD-52

CD-52 represents the certificate of deposit accounts, with the 52 designation representing one account being created for each week of the year. The philosophy behind this system is to replicate receiving steady cash inflow, just as you would when you are employed and receiving a pay check. A weekly periodicity was chosen to allow for maximum flexibility. This also makes it, one of the most impactful components of this plan, due to its ability to replicate normalcy, via its weekly cash injections.

WAR ROOM

The War Room is the nuclear option. It's made to either bring an end to a crisis or allow you to dig your heels in for a protracted campaign. My personal objective here is to have funds to survive for a minimum of 3 years, with no lifestyle changes. I feel I can ride out almost any downturn, with 3 years worth of resources. And when you add in the impact of the ICS, Emergency, and CD-52 accounts, which would all be deployed before touching this one, you're talking about a minimum of 4.5 years of sustainability. This is all without glancing at brokerage, investment, or retirement money.

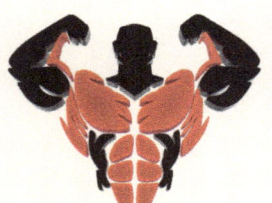

The Anabolic Approach Explained

Gain, Maintain, or Plug the Drain

When starting off, most investors and weightlifters want to **gain** – muscle, wealth, strength, dividends, definition, shares, endurance, safety, attention, status, etc.; take your pick. The investor wants to increase their portfolio value and/or return on investment. The lifter wants to increase their max lift and/or their muscle size. Eventually, the investor will want to **maintain** their portfolio value and preserve their wealth. The lifter will also eventually get to point where they want to maintain their gains and preserve their muscle. For both, the preservation eventuality could be due to some planned interruption, expected downturn, unexpected event, or Time's squeeze. Finally, there will most likely come a time, whether due to injury, old age, or shifting priorities, where the investor and lifter both want to **plug the drain**. They want to slow down the depletion of their resources and degradation of their abilities.

For the investor, maybe they are going through a divorce, have decided to relocate, or have reached retirement and must now use large portions of their wealth. Although it is inevitable that they must utilize their conserved resources, they attempt to do it intelligently and try to slow down the depletion rate, as much as possible. Similarly, the lifter may have sustained an injury, lost competitive fire, or simply gotten older. Here, they know that there will be a decline in performance and musculature, but they endeavor to retard their decline and loss, as much as possible. In both scenarios, the investor and the lifter both still outperform most of their contemporaries. Their eventual declines only result in them sliding backwards to the spot where many of their peers topped out. Plus, if the urge strikes them or circumstances allow, they have the knowledge and experience to resume their work and potentially reverse course, if it suits them.

- **Protein requirements increase, as a person ages.**
- **An already lean person who wants to get shredded has the highest protein requirements of all, regardless of age.**

Money Set

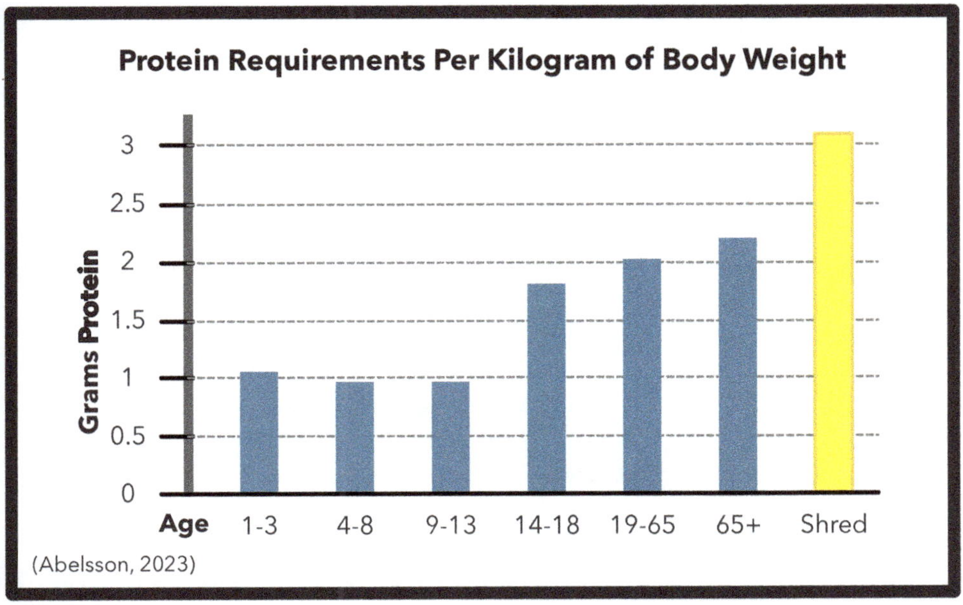
Protein Requirements Per Kilogram of Body Weight
Grams Protein
3
2.5
2
1.5
1
0.5
0
Age
1-3
4-8
9-13
14-18
19-65
65+
Shred
(Abelsson, 2023)

The Vault

The Vault stores restricted use, future need money. Most of your retirement accounts will fall into this category. Account vehicles, such as the 401K, IRA, and HSA all have restrictions and specific rules governing contribution amounts, contribution sources, withdrawal criteria, tax handling, and more. Yes, the money in these accounts is yours, but it is earmarked for very specific purposes (qualified medical expenses, for the HSA, for example) or penalty-free access, based on age (59 ½ years for the 401K, for example).

HSA

The Health Savings Account (HSA) is the most beneficial, tax-efficient, financial vehicle that I know of. Contributions are tax-free, account growth is tax free, withdrawals are tax free for qualified medical expenses, and employers often offer a match contribution. The limitations with it are you must be on a high-deductible health plan and withdrawals must be for qualified medical expenses, to not incur paying taxes and a penalty, before age 65. However, once you turn 65, you can use HSA money to pay for anything you want and you only pay regular taxes but no penalty. This essentially means it has all of the same benefits as a traditional 401K, in this scenario. The HSA also allows you to invest your contributed money, giving you complete control over its portfolio holdings.

401K

The 401K comes in 2 flavors, Traditional and Roth, and typically, employers offer a matching contribution. The difference between these is that the Traditional requires taxes to be paid at withdrawal and the Roth requires taxes to be paid prior to contribution. Although most calculators online and studies show that the difference between their total funds available at withdrawal to be roughly the same, I personally like the Roth. I like the idea of knowing that all of the money I see in the account is the actual money I have available. Also, who knows what kind of funky monkey business is going to be happening with taxes, when it comes time to withdraw. Additionally, the SECURE ACT 2.0 subjects 401K participants to a Required Minimum Distribution (RMD), at age 73 in 2023. Then, it again modifies the RMD age by pushing it back to 75 in 2033. Employee contribution limits are $23,000 if under age 50 and $30,500 if 50 or older. These numbers, for under and over 50 years old, balloon up with an employer match to a maximum of $73,500 and $76,500 annually.

IRAs

The Individual Retirement Account (IRA) shares many similarities with the 401K. However, some key differences are that the IRA is set up and administered by an individual, instead of an employer, there are no match contributions, and the contribution limits are significantly lower. The 2023 IRA contribution limits are $6,500 for those under age 50 and $7,500 for those 50 or older.

TRADITIONAL IRA vs. ROTH IRA

Traditional

- Has No Income Restrictions
- Contributions are Taxed at Withdrawal
- 10% Penalty for Early Withdrawal
- Earnings Taxed at Withdrawal
- Has Required Minimum Distributions

Roth

- Not Available to High Earners
- Funds Are Taxed Before Contribution
- Penalty-Free Contribution Withdrawal
- Earnings are Not Taxed
- The Original Owner Has No RMDs

The Anabolic Approach Explained

Conceit & Humility

The dedicated Anabolic Athlete controls and minimizes conceit, arrogance, and overconfidence. It may not seem like it, but they do. Not in all cases, but often, some of the most powerful athletes you meet will also be the most humble. In fact, most would probably be surprised to know that many of these athletes are actually quite self-conscious, insecure, and uncertain, when it comes to many of their endeavors. Think about it. There is a safety of life and limb issue, for anyone not thinking straight, when moving heavy iron. The powerlifter does not have **The Luxury of Arrogance**, when they have 600 lbs. on their back, as they prepare for a Fanny-to-Fescue squat. They know that the weight is an immutable, ruthless demon that they must respect. They must not put themselves in harm's way with it. It only takes one misstep, one miscalculation, not properly controlling breathing, or not staying tight, in the bottom of the lift, to trigger a catastrophe. Even after they hit a personal record, they can hear the load taunting them by saying, "I dare you to add 20 more lbs. and do it again".

The bodybuilder is extremely vulnerable psychologically, as much of their requested assessments by others is subjective. Some will try to emphasize their strengths, only to have detractors or other competitors ridicule them, by saying, "You would easily be a champion, if you grew those twirling-baton calves and built an actual back". **A lack of confidence** is probably one of the most popular reasons why many begin strength training, in the first place. Many believe increased size and strength will make them tougher, more imposing, and keep those who would harm them at bay. They do this only to find out that no matter how strong they get and how big they become, **it's never enough**. Eventually, though, through consistency and dedication, most find balance. They tap into the confidence that they sought, for so very long, not because of their size and their strength, but because they finally KNOW themselves. They know what they are about, what they are built of inside, capable of doing, and willing to do. And, now, even if some of those muscles and some of that strength leaves them, as it inevitably will, it doesn't matter, as they are whole.

Money Set

_____
_____
_____
_____
_____
_____
_____
_____
_____
_____
_____

Be pliable or you won't be prudent. Become more humble as the market goes your way. It is not prudent to buy when you think the bottom has been reached. It is better to wait and see, and buy too late. It is not prudent to wait for the top of the market to sell—it is better to sell too soon.

– Bernard Baruch
(Grant, 1983)

Builder Box

Add Structural Protection

Once you've eliminated your debt and shored up the Battle Box and Vault, the Builder Box can begin to take on serious mass. This is where you can begin to significantly extend your fiscal capabilities. Every single account category in the Builder Box has **principle preservation**, coupled with **asset value appreciation**, as its core tenet. Your balance should always be more than your cost basis (what you initially contributed), and once assets are active, they should grow and compound, with minimal tending. Now is the time to extend and strengthen your fiscal moat.

SWAN

Coined by financial analyst, Brad Thomas, SWAN stands for Sleep Well At Night. These are financial vehicles that you consider to be very stable, offer a return that at a minimum outpaces inflation, and hopefully keeps pace with the S&P 500. One of the easiest ways to keep pace with the S&P 500 is to invest in an index fund that tracks the S&P 500. For me, SWANs that are index based are more attractive than individual companies. I consider these foundational accounts. Other entries would include blue chip funds/companies that have significant market share, a large market cap, a wide operational moat, and positive-trending historical data.

GROWTH

Growth stocks tend to experience more volatility than index based funds. They tend to have higher (Price-To-Earnings) P/E ratios but also offer higher potential returns. Growth vehicles may or may not pay a dividend.

DIVIDEND

Dividend stocks pay a portion of earnings back to investors in the form of dividends. **A company has several things they can do with their profits: pay down debt, buy back their own stock shares, invest in their own company, invest in or buy another company, or distribute it back to investors.** Here, I define profits as all of the cash generated by and available from operations, minus any mandatory capital expenditures.

RISKY

Risky stocks are unproven or speculative securities that have potential to offer significant returns but also have significant limitations, weaknesses, hazards, or uncertainties that must be factored in. Be cautious, here.

FOOLISH

Foolish stocks would be either passion projects or things you just have a "feeling" about that may not be fundamentally sound. This is a low form of gambling, and you are essentially playing the lottery. However, it is not gambling proper. Actual gambling money needs to come from the Throw Away account, but this money here needs to be intelligently allocated and meticulously tracked.

CRYPTOCURRENCY

This is soaking your money in gasoline and throwing a lit match on it with the hopes that there is a bar of gold hidden within the ashes. I believe crypto, or some permutation of it, to be a cornerstone in the future of finance. I'm just not certain how it will look. Still, I think it is prudent for most to delve into this arena, to understand how it works. But, novices need to do so with extreme caution. There are many ways to lose your money with crypto. Exchanges get hacked, and they sometimes are shutdown. Tokens are treated like cash, so once you authorize the transaction, it's gone; you'd better be sure.

The Hodgerian CD-52 Method

To further expound on the concept, CD-52 represents 52 certificate of deposit accounts, with one account created for each week of the year. The philosophy behind this system is to replicate receiving steady cash inflow, as you would when you are employed and receiving a pay check. A weekly periodicity was chosen to allow for maximum flexibility. A bank issued Certificate of Deposit, or CD, is a time-bound deposit where you agree to leave your money deposited for an agreed upon time frame, or term, in exchange for a guaranteed interest rate. For a traditionally structured CD, early withdrawal will result in a penalty, as well as forfeiture of any earned interest. Opening a CD is easy with the convenience afforded by online banking and can easily be setup and funded in less than 5 minutes, with some banks. The steps to setup are as easy as selecting an FDIC insured bank (very important, so your money is guaranteed to survive a bank failure), selecting an available term, agreeing to the interest rate and stipulations, funding the account, which is usually just a transfer from another account to the CD account, if it is being done through the same bank, and authorizing the action to commence. And, that's it. Done.

Although there are several types of CDs with various features that may appeal to some buyers, I will focus on the simplest form which is the traditional CD, for this example. Once the CD matures, you have a few options. You can close the account

52 Certificate of Deposit Accounts

Create 1 account every week for a year. When each CD reaches maturity, roll the principle and interest over and add to it. Continue this until you have at least 1 year's worth of living expenses or need to invoke a Battle Plan.

and simply withdraw the funds. Or, you can perform what is called a "Rollover", where you leave the account open. With a Rollover, you have the ability to change the term, leave the existing funds, or add more funds to it with whatever the new rate is. Some of you may have heard of a CD Ladder. A CD Ladder is a staggered allocation method where you separate (usually equal sized) deposits by some predetermined interval. A common CD Ladder, for example, is the 5-Year Ladder where 5 separate CDs with a 5-Year term are created over the course of 5 years. Or more simply, every year for 5 years, buy a new CD that has a 5 year term. **I don't know of any money managers who would advise you to invest in CDs to acquire massive wealth.** CDs reduce your liquidity, since they are time-bound, and if interest rates rise, it will result in a larger Inflation Wealth Gap. And even if rates don't rise, the interest for CDs is somewhat low, which means the APY will be low. Plus, there are penalties for early withdrawal.

So with all of this said, why am I recommending CDs for strong consideration within a financial strategy. Well, the idea here is that CDs, at least for me, are meant to be used in a very specific way for very specific reasons. I use CDs as a type of Slush

Fund but not the illegal kind where Mr. Bad-Guy McNasty does Dastardly Deeds and Dirty Things with it. I call it a Slush Fund in the sense that it is not completely liquid and it is not completely frozen – it sits somewhere in between. Good uses for a CD for me are for money I'm saving up for a specific future purchase, an investment, a War Chest Fund injection, or as a Holding Tank for a cyclical obligation like taxes. The CD-52 Method takes the CD and the CD Ladder one step further, and I'll cover that in more detail in a bit. Now, for the actual CD-52 Method, I must admit that I haven't seen anybody advocating for this specific method of investing or Money Management that uses 52 CDs, and I have searched the web looking for it. But, just because I haven't seen it, it doesn't mean somebody else hasn't said buy one CD a week for a year (or even 1 a day for a year – but that would be CD-365 and overkill *teehee*)! Of course, this may mean that the reason nobody else has said it is because it's a stupid thing to do. But, I have my reasons. So, this may not be for you, but as with this and everything else, your choices are your own. The CD-52 Method I use is very simple. Starting from scratch, my protocol is to:

Open One CD Account, with a 1-Year Term, Every FRI, Every Week, for 1 Year.

After that, the 52 account target is reached. From here, as each CD reaches maturity, I'll make a determination on whether to withdraw the cash and the accrued interest, rollover the existing cash and accrued interest into the same fund, or roll it all over and add more money to it. When rolling over, a new, 1-year term is established, and it will have whatever the new interest rate is. The obvious desire here is to keep rolling over and adding to each CD, until your goal is reached.

Now, once the goal is reached, something magical happens. Even if you stop the contributions, the CDs should at a minimum match and will most likely outpace inflation over time, if you are using a high interest CD. I use Ally Bank, as they are one of the best Swiss Army Knife type of banks, in that they can do pretty much everything from bill pay to CDs and from retirement to investing. And, they consistently provide outstanding rates. When an Ally Bank CD matures, they add a 0.05% Loyalty Reward to the new term's interest rate. This means that a 3.00% interest rate becomes 3.05%. The current annual inflation result, for the 12 months ending JUN 2024, is 2.97% (McMahon, 2024). The average interest rate I received from Ally Bank, which includes the Loyalty Reward for that same time period, was 4.84%. This means that, on average, with a fully funded CD-52 setup, these CDs outpaced inflation by 1.87%. If an economy remains mostly stable and mostly healthy, aside from the occasional anomaly, interest rates should always exceed inflation. This means the buying power of this solution should match its economic reality in perpetuity. I have performed this same exercise several times before, and it has given similar results every time.

The Hodgerian CD-52 Method (Cont.)

You can use an online bank like Ally Bank that allows you to create multiple CD accounts, for free, with no minimum deposits. To get started with CD-52, open one CD account each week for 52 weeks. Fund each with whatever you can that makes sense for you. If you get paid every other week, split the weekly allocation into two equal sizes for that cycle. If you get paid twice monthly, you might need to adjust the split to account for uneven weeks, but it doesn't matter. **The amount is secondary to establishing and sticking to the process, until you have achieved your goal.** To simplify it a little more, if you reasoned that you could contribute $40 for a given month to the CD 52 Method, you would fund each CD for that month with $10 each. If for the next month, you reason that you could contribute $100 for the month, you would fund each CD with $25 for that month. If that month has 5 deposit days instead of 4, you would deposit $20 each week.

As a side note, make sure that you deposit on the same day each week – don't do it on THU one week MON the next and SUN the one after that. That is just going to make things messy and create psychic noise. Personally, I like to deposit on FRIs, and I like to keep the amounts as close to the same as possible, so that the income is consistent should I need to activate a rolling withdrawal protocol. By keeping the day of deposit and amounts consistent, it further ensures that the CD-52 Method becomes, essentially, just another bill or budget line item that I have gotten used to that causes minimal impact. Ultimately though, each person can choose their own rules. Even though I like to try to keep the amounts the same, it's much more important to actually save whatever you can each cycle, rather than keeping the amounts consistent. It's fine to contribute $2.00, if that's all you have, one week. Eventually, you will be able to adjust the contribution amounts to even things out in subsequent rounds. What I mean by this is if the starting balances for a cycle are $10, $20, $10, and $30 for progressive weeks in a particular month, during that same month for the following year's cycle, you could allocate $25, $15, $25, and $5 for each week for the new month, to make all of the balances the same. But, again, I can't stress this part enough, it's still much more important to save what you can as you go, rather than keeping the balances exactly the same.

After several years with a steady job, discipline, and consistent contributions, maybe you could get each of your CDs up to $100, or $300, or maybe even $500. Monthly that means you could count on $400, $1200, or $2000 respectively, without fail, like it was a pay check. Annually, this means if you had to activate the protocol, that would be $5200, $15600, or $26000 respectively – and that's not including any other monies from other sources. The magic goal would be $1000. That would

result in $52000 saved and ready.

Incidentally, your establishing a $1000 or $2000 Emergency Fund can be done in concert with this method; you would just put minimal amounts in the CDs, until the Emergency Fund was fully hydrated. This method is especially beneficial for people with limited funds, poor people, undisciplined people, or people who don't know what they want to do with their money, but they know they just don't want to keep blowing it on stupid stuff, while they figure out how to deploy Smart Money.

CD-52 Account List Example

CDs	Current	YTD Interest	Matures	APY
CD-01:04JAN2030	$12.34	$0.14	JAN 04, 2031	4.55%
CD-02:11JAN2030	$113.13	$0.87	JAN 11, 2031	4.55%
CD-03:18JAN2030	$13.18	$0.12	JAN 18, 2031	4.50%
CD-04:25JAN2030	$144.76	$0.81	JAN 25, 2031	4.50%
CD-05:01FEB2030	$215.58	$1.02	FEB 01, 2031	4.90%
CD-06:08FEB2030	$15.72	$0.09	FEB 08, 2031	4.90%
CD-07:15FEB2030	$15.58	$0.07	FEB 15, 2031	4.90%

CDs 8 - 45 Are Listed In This Missing Section

CDs	Current	YTD Interest	Matures	APY
CD-46:15NOV2030	$16.83	$0.76	NOV 15, 2031	4.90%
CD-47:22NOV2030	$18.09	$0.82	NOV 22, 2031	4.90%
CD-48:29NOV2030	$516.58	$22.42	NOV 29, 2031	4.90%
CD-49:06DEC2030	$19.35	$0.97	DEC 06, 2031	5.30%
CD-50:13DEC2030	$92.17	$4.58	DEC 13, 2031	5.30%
CD-51:20DEC2030	$106.67	$5.48	DEC 20, 2031	5.30%
CD-52:27DEC2030	$23.88	$1.14	DEC 27, 2031	5.30%
Total	**$2,196.83**	**$76.46**		

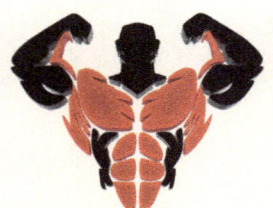

The Anabolic Approach Explained

Willingly Give Up Comfort – No Whining

Crossfitters, bodybuilders, powerlifters, Olympic lifters, home gym warriors, and strongmen all sacrifice. Some give up more than others, but they all get cut deep, to the bone, via immolation. All of this is done with no guarantees and, sometimes, not even the probability of reward, yet they endeavor on. Many choose jobs, relationships, and living arrangements that align with their goals. Sometimes, for the truly driven, they are forced to do without even the barest of essentials. I've known of several strength athletes who existed in various states of homelessness, to pursue their dreams. I saw an interview with Robby Robinson, the Black Prince, recalling how he took a one-way trip to California to become a bodybuilding champion. He had no backup plan. In another interview, I saw Tom Platz relay how he was living in his van to save money, so he could eat and train. Strength athletes sleep on couches, in cars, in tents, and wherever else they need to, in pursuit of their elusive dreams.

From a fiscal perspective, this same type of **sacrifice** may be required, for you to keep making progress. You may find yourself living at or beneath the poverty level, to achieve your financial goals. You may need to skip meals, go without heat or cooling, wear tattered clothing, live in dilapidated housing, and use unsatisfactory transportation. All of that, and more, may be necessary to pay down your high interest credit card, eliminate a car payment, or build an Emergency Fund. The strength athlete is able to effortless do all of those things, aside from the skipping meals part (eating properly is essential for them), as they are built to endure and apply effort to these types of long-term goals. The only thing most lifters are missing is an inspiring target and a solid plan on how to proceed. And once they improve their situation and figure out that they can oftentimes do both, build muscle and build wealth, simultaneously, they become unstoppable. For anyone who finds themselves homeless, like I was, create a plan to change your circumstances, and then get to work by taking action. When you do, you'll discover that **you didn't fail, but instead, you simply found one more thing that couldn't stop you**.

Money Set

Vehicular Homelessness Rises

There is no U.S. state where a full-time, minimum-wage worker can afford the rent, for a modest two-bedroom apartment. The average minimum-wage worker must work 113 hours (2.8 full-time jobs) per week to afford a two bedroom rental, at the fair market value of $1,670. (NLIHC, 2024)

Story Time: CD-52

Ideally, CD-52 money is not to be used for any other purchase that could be planned for or otherwise saved for – not the new clothes you want, or the muscle car, or the exotic trip, or the cell phone, or the Sig Sauer 10mm, etc. This money will eventually become an extension of your Fiscal War Chest and supplement your march towards true **Wealth and Independence.**

Now, the real reason I created this CD-52 Method for My Self is that I found myself poor, unemployed, and homeless for a while, on two separate occasions, in the 1990s. From time to time, I was miserable trying to keep my body clean, by washing up where ever I could. I tried to always choose lockable, single user bathrooms at gas stations or big box stores, or I would periodically get one of those free, 2-week gym memberships, so I could REALLY get clean in their showers. When you don't have a place and you're ducking and dodging around areas you're not supposed to be, that gym shower is luxurious. I also remember sometimes being very hungry to where I would just hibernate to make it go away; **I would have a nap for a snack and sleep for dinner – Ha!** A side effect of this is that, to this day, I will go all day without eating anything at all and sometimes only eat my first piece of food, after I've gotten home from work (and occasionally, I'll skip a day, altogether). I was essentially doing intermittent fasting out of necessity, before it was cool. But during my homeless and hungry time, it wasn't that cool, since I was doing it because I had no choice. Even so, every so often I would get a hotel room, and it would be the best thing ever! **EVER!!!** I remember it being winter time and me sleeping in the back seat of my 1972 Nova (I guess I wasn't really hardcore homeless, since I had a car, but there are levels to The Misery). When you've pulled several weeks worth of freezing nights balled up in the back seat of a drafty Chevy Nova, and decide to get a hotel room, at the Beach, on an upper floor, facing the ocean – man, you feel like a million bucks! I can still remember being on the 12th floor of the Days Inn, peacefully gazing at that roiling ocean. Snugglemalized under the covers, I had the heater cranking and the patio door broadly ajar all evening, so I could fully hear the primordial growl of the sea. The erratic mix of crisp, nocturnal air, dry, hotel heat, and deep, ocean rumble lullabied me to sleep – beddy-bye, all night long. Those little things meant so much. In many ways, **this was the best time of my life**.

I bought a bunch of grocery store food and even a couple of things, from some fast food joints. I was able to clean myself up really good, watch some TV, and actually fall asleep. And, I binged on ALL of it. I think at one point I took 5 showers in a single day, just because I could. And, anybody who knows me knows that I hardly ever actually sleep, but in those days, at that time, in that hotel room were the times I remember doing it. I can't stress enough how having someplace warm and safe, with a hot plate of food, when you've been cold and distressed, can comfort you, when you're going through a rough patch. I always told myself that if I ever found myself in a bad way again, I would have something to help me make it through. Being able to count on a certain amount of money each and every week, for an entire year, can do that. There is no place, person, or institution I can run to, when hard times and misery comes (and I wouldn't turn to it, even if I could). I only have me to protect me. **The CD-52 Method was built solely to give me confidence, comfort, and contentment, in case I fell on hard times again – and for nothing else.**

Homelessness Classifications

Don't fool yourself into thinking that becoming homeless is something that can't happen to you. In fact, many of you may have already experienced a level of it without knowing it. There are 4 main categories of homelessness, according to the United Nations Economic Commission for Europe, of which the United States is a member:

1. **Literally Homeless** - Individual or family who lacks a fixed, regular, and adequate nighttime residence

2. **Imminent Risk of Homelessness** - An individual or family who will imminently lose their primary nighttime residence within 14 days

3. **Homeless Under Other Federal Statutes** - Has made 2 or more moves or have not had a lease, ownership interest in permanent housing, during the 60 days

4. **Fleeing/Attempting to Flee Domestic Violence** - Has no other residence and lacks the resources or support networks to obtain other permanent housing

Other Homelessness Examples

(HUD Exchange, n.d.)

SHELTER/MISSION
Organized shelter for individuals experiencing homelessness

ABANDONED BUILDINGS
Buildings that have been decommissioned, by their owners.

VEHICLES
Any untethered auto (cars, trucks, campers, vans, heavy machinery, etc.).

HOTELS
Temporary, provisional, managed accommodations.

UNSHELTERED OUTDOORS
Low to no protection from environment or elements.

TENTS/ENCAMPMENTS
Moderate protection from environment or elements.

I Remember When It Was Me

Sometimes when I give money to folks begging, people say that I'm being taken or that it's a scam. It might be. But, that's not my problem. Whether the person buys the gas they said they needed or they buy alcohol or some other substance, I did my part, even if it was small. It's hard to say what pebbles are causing pain, how many holes are in the socks, or where the leather has rubbed feet raw, until you've walked in another man's shoes. That bottle of spirits might be the only comfort they get for the night; it might also be the thing that prevents a desperation assault on someone you care about, later that day.

FISICALITY

SECTION 5

CRUISING

Utilizing Tools and Tactics

Now that you've created the plan and gathered the data, let's aggregate it and pretty everything up, to make it easy to read, use, and manage. The objective here is to end up with an information dense resource that will be efficient to use. Frequently fumbling around, sifting through papers, and trying to find critical information is something that will minimize your effectiveness. Keep your myriad records with your archive, but all of the actual management should be done using our created resource. Taking the time now to build a proper system and resource will not only make things easier but will, dare I say it, make it enjoyable. Once you've got everything dialed in, you find that your time requirement, in a regular month, to manage all of your finances, may be as little as 20 minutes, because all you are really doing most months is recording your incoming cash and then distributing it, according to the plan. If you automate this, it will be even quicker. Personally, I don't like to automate these things, as I like to maintain a pleasurably banal intimacy with my Money Management. But, I know many people like automated transactions, so it's still an option for you, if you're comfortable with it. **There are 5 components, in the basic tracking setup: Fisicality Ledger, Social Security Earnings History Tracker, Net Worth Tracker, PRIME Calculations Worksheet, and Accounts List.**

The Fisicality Ledger

The Fisicality Ledger is built with 12 months of data projections, based on historical actuals, updated expectations, and calculated projections (several months are hidden, in the example). Accounts and identities are listed in the ITEM column. Items that are marked under the CC (Credit Card) column are payed with a CC, but their totals are not added to a CC in the sheet; it's settled at bill paying time. I haven't come up with a more graceful way to do this in the spreadsheet, just yet. Incoming funds are tracked in the dark background, in the upper section, and Outgoing funds are tracked in the white background, in the lower section. The active month's outgoing funds expectation for each item is highlighted in yellow. The active month is marked as "OPEN", once actual amounts are verified and bills are staged to be paid. The red active tracking block is shaded to assist with tasks, such as double checking values, setting up the payment, or verifying planned payments, as needed. Once all line items have been satisfied, the month's column is marked as "CLOSED", and the next month is selected, in the upper right corner, which now marks the new selected month with a yellow background. Monthly totals are tallied at the bottom of each column and reflects the balance of all Incoming and Outgoing money. Actual and Projected totals are tallied in the last 2 columns, on the far right. The Saved and Wasted percentages and amounts are tallied, based on the ITEMs you select, for each category. For instance, in this example, SAVED contains Rolling CD-52, Battle Box, Emergency, Plans, War Chest, and Vest. WASTED contains all credit cards, regardless of what was purchased on them. As all worthy and justified spend is tracked in the spreadsheet with payment sometimes administered through the credit card, it's purpose is already accounted for. All justified purchases need to be accounted for, on the spreadsheet. Anything not accounted for is considered waste.

FISICALITY MAIN This is the workhorse of the system, once everything is setup. Everything, all other resources, feed into this component, in some way. I tend to review this, every time I open the sheet.

2030 FISICALITY LEDGER						JUL
ITEM			JUN	JUL	AUG	ACTUAL	PROJECTION
Source 1			4,408.18	0.00	0.00	15,591.71	15,591.71
Source 2			0.00	0.00	0.00	0.00	0.00
Source 3			0.00	0.00	0.00	0.00	0.00
INCOMING TOTAL			4,408.18	0.00	0.00	15,591.71	15,591.71
ITEM	I	CC	CLOSED	OPEN			
Big Bank CD | Rolling 52			0.00	0.00	0.00	0.00	0.00
Big Bank CHK | Bill Payer			0.00	0.00	0.00	0.00	0.00
Big Bank CHK | Tactical			0.00	0.00	0.00	0.00	0.00
Big Bank SAV | Battle Box			0.00	0.00	0.00	0.00	0.00
Big Bank SAV | Emergency			0.00	0.00	0.00	0.00	0.00
Big Bank SAV | Plans			0.00	0.00	0.00	0.00	0.00
Big Bank SAV | War Chest			0.00	0.00	0.00	0.00	0.00
Credit Card | Chaste			0.00	0.00	0.00	0.00	0.00
Credit Card | Finderer			0.00	0.00	0.00	0.00	0.00
Credit Card | Crappital Wah			1,500.00	2,500.00	500.00	10,125.00	12,625.00
Coms | ABC & T			31.03	0.00	0.00	276.03	276.03
Coms | Megaphone Cellular		X	0.00	180.00	0.00	255.00	330.00
Ins | Highco			160.00	0.00	68.60	160.00	548.60
Tax | City Property Tax			791.02	0.00	0.00	791.02	791.02
Tax | Federal Annual			30.18	0.00	0.00	30.18	30.18
Tax | State Annual		X	0.00	0.00	0.00	50.00	50.00
Util | Real Estate Tax			1,460.51	1,460.51	1,460.51	10,223.57	17,526.12
Util | Water			0.00	0.00	0.00	0.00	0.00
Util | Power			0.00	0.00	0.00	0.00	0.00
Util | Sanitation			0.00	0.00	0.00	0.00	0.00
Util | Natural Gas		X	0.00	0.00	0.00	0.00	0.00
Vest | Investing			0.00	0.00	0.00	115.79	115.79
PRIME | All Debt Payoff			150.00	170.00	250.00	1,135.00	1,985.00
PRIME | Name			225.44	0.00	0.00	661.77	889.76
PRIME | Name			60.00	80.00	150.00	440.00	940.00
PRIME | Name			0.00	0.00	0.00	0.00	0.00
PRIME | Name			0.00	0.00	0.00	0.00	0.00
OUTGOING TOTAL			4,408.18	4,390.51	2,429.11	24,263.36	36,107.50
BALANCE			0.00	-4,390.51	-2,429.11	-8,671.65	-20,515.79
• $ SAVED			0.00	0.00	0.00	0.00	0
• % SAVED			0.00%	0.00%	0.00%	0.00%	0.00%
• $ WASTED			1500	2500	500	10125	12625
• % WASTED			34.03%	56.94%	20.58%	41.73%	34.97%

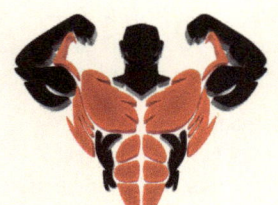

The Anabolic Approach Explained

Impact of Intelligent Planning

It takes intentional planning, monitoring, tracking, and adjustments to be successful with Money Management and Anabolic endeavors. When starting with either, a few areas of consideration are:

MONEY MATTERS	ANABOLIC ACTIVITIES
• Portfolio Selection	• Exercise Selection
• Investment Approach	• Rep Scheme
• Asset Research	• Rest Time Between Sets
• Trading Frequency	• Workout Frequency
• Capital Return Targets	• Intensity Targets
• Financial Self-Study	• Nutrition
• Performance Reviews	• Rest
• Dry Powder Accumulation	• Hydration
• Asset Exploration	• Supplementation

Now, to be honest, there are many other activities that people engage in that also require similar attention. The difference here is that the Anabolic athlete (or investor) willingly puts themselves at risk in a meaningful way. They are putting their bodies and well-being at risk, in a manner where errors, miscalculations, or accidents will draw real blood, cause real injury, or result in chronic damage. Proper strength training is very safe, however when things go bad, they go bad to the extreme. There is not much middle ground. This is similar to what a boxer, at any level, would experience, as their miscalculations result in getting punched in the face. That's much different than the mistake the office manager makes at their corporate job, where faux pas are overlooked, disregarded, and smoothed over, After all, we can let the shareholders pay the price for those mistakes. And by the way, congrats on your big raise; and you can keep the change too, you Filthy Animal ➡ unapologetic channeling of "Home Alone", channeling James Cagney, in "Angels With Dirty Faces" (Gatollari, 2018).

Money Set

_____

_____

_____

_____

_____

_____

_____

_____

_____

_____

_____

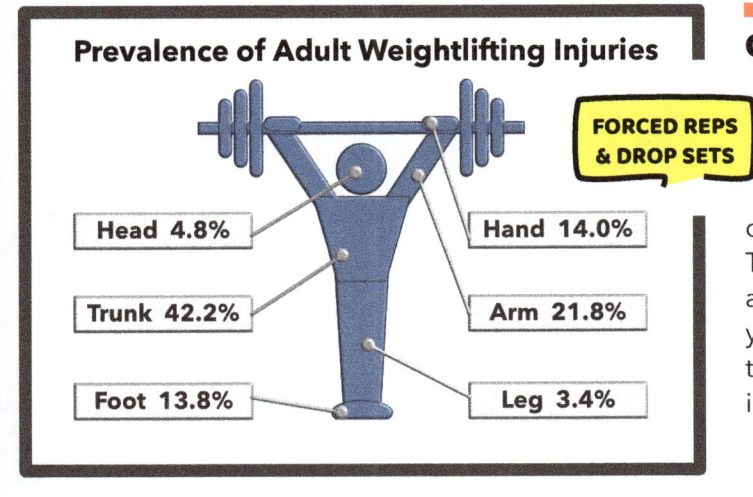

Prevalence of Adult Weightlifting Injuries

FORCED REPS & DROP SETS

Head 4.8%

Hand 14.0%

Trunk 42.2%

Arm 21.8%

Foot 13.8%

Leg 3.4%

OUCH!

Learning how to workout around injuries is critical for success. The old joke is, athletics is what you do to pass the time in between injuries.

Social Security and Net Worth Trackers

I really enjoy seeing macroview data, like this Social Security Earnings Report. It really puts everything in perspective, when you can pull back and see clearly from 1,000 feet above, what looked to be all jumbled up, when you were up close. I really like working with big chunks of money, whenever I can. Everything is just so clear and blatantly obvious. I'll sometimes create a fake bill that I pour money into. I pretend it's for a high interest CC, for a phantom company that I created. I do all of this, just so I can have a big chunk of money to manage regularly. It changes my thinking. This is probably one of the reasons why people who don't have money don't think like people who do have and understand money (some people have it and still don't understand it). Your perspective shifts, when your available resources drastically shift up or down, but the person who has been on either side of the shift is able to draw from that experience.

For the example to the right, what guidance do you think this person would provide to their 30-year-ago self, with this knowledge? If you could go back in time, with the knowledge you have now, and have a conversation with your 18-year-old self AND present them with all of the money they would make over the next 30 years, as a lump sum, with the caveat that they would not get another penny from anything else, aside from the money generated from the money they were now getting, would you give them a plan to maximize it? Would you tell them to take it? I would. **It would essentially be like winning the lottery, except I would have a plan.**

2030 SOCIAL SECURITY EARNINGS		
YEAR	EARNINGS	MEDICARE EARNINGS
1992	1,100	1,100
1993	428	428
1994	788	788
1995	855	855
1996	814	814
1997	1,395	1,395
1998	9,177	9,177
1999	7,219	7,219
2000	14,742	14,742
2001	11,504	11,504
2002	17,407	17,407
2003	30,205	30,205
2004	25,712	25,712
2005	16,982	16,982
2006	21,858	21,858
2007	34,872	34,872
2008	38,144	38,144
2009	41,668	41,668
2010	42,140	42,140
2011	48,227	48,227
2012	62,985	62,985
2013	70,255	70,255
2014	82,572	82,572
2015	86,951	86,951
2016	88,122	88,122
2017	86,525	86,525
2018	91,427	91,427
2019	93,810	93,810
2020	94,100	94,100
2021	112,536	112,536
2022	116,222	116,222
2023	127,409	127,409
2024	128,565	156,872
2025	131,741	158,421
2026	136,018	160,855
2027	22,164	22,164
2028	114,982	114,982
2029	34,581	34,581
2030	147,363	179,648
YEARLY AVERAGE	$55,948	
LIFETIME TOTAL	$2,126,026	

Benefits are calculated using the 35 highest earning years.

For the most part, how much you have in your bank account is meaningless. I often hear people discuss how much they have in this account, or in that stock, or how much their house costs, or what they paid for their boat. It's all drivel. The question to ask is, "What is your Net Worth?". That's all that matters. This does not mean that having access to immediate cash or that having access to a line of credit to extend your capabilities is not important. They are just not as important, when assessing one's true and total fiscal strength. The nitty-gritty of the thing is to track your Net Worth. If that's rising annually, you're on track. It's easy to be fooled by an infrequent, large return. And, it's also easy to let bad habits meander about, behind the scenes, not account for them, and adopt a false confidence or false sense of security that crumbles under duress. Again, activity that is not tracked cannot be measured. And, that which is not measured cannot be intelligently managed. This can lead to any big return you receive getting washed away, in one fell swoop, by the massive bill you'll run up on your "Cancun Clam Capture" trip.

Although it is acceptable to do, I'm not a staunch believer in adding things to the asset column that are not tangible or realized, generally speaking. I exclude most non-liquid or hard to liquidate assets. Just because somebody owes you money, it doesn't mean you're going to get it, so I suggest only accounting for Assets that give you high confidence in hitting a liquidation target. Securities and their portfolio values fluctuate over short periods of time, but you should see a steady rise over longer time frames. For example, in the chart below, individual values fluctuate, but the general trend from the previous, end-of-year value is upwards.

NET WORTH TRACKER Simply put, your Net Worth represents the value of everything you have minus everything you owe. However, aside from the known, estimated dubious value of certain assets, such as a car, boat, house, or land, I tend to only include securities, bank accounts, bonds, cash, etc. in my asset list. You have no way of knowing what the true market value of your Richie Rich comic book collection is, or if somebody is going to want it, or how long it will take to sell it. This record is updated monthly.

2030 NET WORTH								
ACCOUNT	2029 EOY	JAN	FEB	MAR	OCT	NOV	DEC	
401K - 1	195,799	196,132	196,464	196,797	0	0	0	
401K - 2	224,199	230,020	235,840	244,832		0	0	
Big Bank Battle Box	1,433	1,000	1,000	1,000		0	0	
Big Bank Builder Box	7,026	7,065	7,065	7,000		0	0	
Big Bank CD I CD-52	16,547	17,281	17,424	17,654	0	0	0	
Big Bank Vault	2,000	2,000	2,000	2,000	0	0	0	
Big Broker Investments - 1	7,744	7,654	7,512	5,565	0	0	0	
Big Broker Investments - 2	66,623	67,895	68,542	66,878		0	0	
Crypto Wallet	4,513	4,613	4,682	4,721		0	0	
Mortgage	-181,536	-181,166	-180,805	-180,445		0	0	
Mortgage Value	255,000	255,000	255,000	255,000	0	0	0	
Old Folks HSA - 1	22,957	22,967	22,967	22,967	0	0	0	
Old Folks HSA - 2	17,792	18,181	18,813	19,444		0	0	
ROLLUP - 1	281,260	288,513	295,801	306,282	0	0	0	
ROLLUP - 2	80,880	82,162	82,736	79,164	0	0	0	
IGNORE MORTAGE DATA	362,140	370,675	378,537	385,446	0	0	0	
LIQUID NET WORTH	333,171	341,840	349,212	357,437	0	0	0	
TOTAL NET WORTH	640,097	648,642	656,504	663,413	0	0	0	

PRIME Calculations Tool

The PRIME Calculations Sheet is where you make the decisions for how you will allocate all funds not consumed by the Razor (which to reiterate, includes all of your minimum obligations). **This unconsumed money, post-Razor, is the After Shave.** Ultimately, my assertion is that everyone would be better served to eliminate all non-productive debt, especially high cost, revolving debt. However, eliminating amortized home and fixed auto loan debt is also important. My reasoning here is simple. These debt buckets typically hang around so long, for most people, that they become normalized. They become expected and acceptable. But, they are not acceptable to me. Ask yourself, what could you do with the money you pay on rent or mortgage each month? Of course, I know some of the arguments against paying a mortgage down, as fast as possible: you could get a higher return in the XYZ market, you'll miss out on the tax savings, or you're going to negatively impact your quality of life. To that I say that a higher return is not guaranteed, the tax savings aren't that great, and finally, my quality of life and peace of mind would be greatly enhanced, by intelligently living beneath my means and eliminating all anxiety associated with a mortgage. The mortgage example is just that, an example. But, all debt, especially high interest debt should be aggressively eliminated. However, if you decide to make some other category or item the PRIME, you easily can; it is a modular system. However, using my recommended, initial PRIME of All Debt Elimination, let's review the worksheet. The Accounts section lists out each group. The main section lists out the percentage-based, distribution amounts, paired with its corresponding dollar amount. Each of the PRIME sections are prioritized, from left to right, in the order that makes sense for your thesis. As in the example, the basic order I recommend is:

PRIME CALCULATIONS The PRIME Sheet lets you know how much money to allocate to each section, based on the percentages you established. This record is reviewed monthly and updated, as needed, quarterly.

ACCOUNTS	ALL DEBT		BATTLE BOX		VAULT		BUILDER BOX		OPERATIONS		CONSTRICTOR	
AFTER SHAVE	100	100%	100	100%	100	100%	100	100%	100	100%	100	100%
ALL DEBT PAYOFF	80.00	80%									20.00	20%
Item 1	64.00	80%										
Item 2	16.00	20%										
BATTLE BOX	8.00	8%	50.00	50%							20.00	20%
ICS	4.00	50%	25.00	50%							10.00	50%
CD-52	2.00	25%	12.50	25%							5.00	25%
Emergency	1.50	19%	9.38	19%							3.75	19%
War Room	0.50	6%	3.13	6%							1.25	6%
THE VAULT	5.00	5%	25.00	25%	50.00	50%					35.00	35%
HSA	2.50	50%	12.50	50%	25.00	50%					17.50	50%
401K	1.50	30%	7.50	30%	15.00	30%					10.50	30%
IRA	1.00	20%	5.00	20%	10.00	20%					7.00	20%
BUILDER BOX	4.00	4%	15.00	15%	30.00	30%	80.00	80%			40.00	40%
SWAN	1.20	30%	4.50	30%	9.00	30%	24.00	30%			12.00	30%
Growth	0.88	22%	3.30	22%	6.60	22%	17.60	22%			8.80	22%
Dividend	0.88	22%	3.30	22%	6.60	22%	17.60	22%			8.80	22%
Risky	0.52	13%	1.95	13%	3.90	13%	10.40	13%			5.20	13%
Foolish	0.36	9%	1.35	9%	2.70	9%	7.20	9%			3.60	9%
Crypto	0.16	4%	0.60	4%	1.20	4%	3.20	4%			1.60	4%
OPERATIONS BOX	3.00	3%	10.00	10%	20.00	20%	20.00	20%	100.00	100%	5.00	5%
Plans	2.10	70%	7.00	70%	14.00	70%	14.00	70%	70.00	70%	3.50	70%
Throw Away	0.90	30%	3.00	30%	6.00	30%	6.00	30%	30.00	30%	1.50	30%
VALIDATION												
$	%	$	%	$	%	$	%	$	%	$	%
100	100%	100	100%	100	100%	100	100%	100	100%	100	100%
80.00	100%	0.00	0%	0.00	0%	0.00	0%	0.00	0%	0.00	0%
8.00	100%	50.00	100%	0.00	0%	0.00	0%	0.00	0%	20.00	100%
5.00	100%	25.00	100%	50.00	100%	0.00	0%	0.00	0%	35.00	100%
4.00	100%	15.00	100%	30.00	100%	80.00	100%	0.00	0%	40.00	100%
3.00	100%	10.00	100%	20.00	100%	20.00	100%	100.00	100%	5.00	100%

(ADP) Get Rid of Crazy Debt → (Battle Box) Prepare for Bad Times → (Vault) Build Long-Term Resources → (Builder Box) Increase Diversity → (Operations Box) Scratch Itches, within the 3-Month Constrictor Window.

As the requirements for each PRIME category are satisfied, it is deactivated, and the subsequent category becomes the new PRIME. Let's do a practical walk-through. In the ADP PRIME column, the example uses $100 as the After Shave (the amount left over after the Razor has "shaved" off surplus). Of this, 80% ($80.00) is allocated to ADP, 8% ($8.00) to the Battle Box, 5% ($5.00) to The Vault, 4% ($4.00) to the Builder Box, and 3% ($3.00) to the Operations Box. Those section total amounts are broken down further, like so. Of the $80.00 in ADP, it is distributed among the category items, starting with the debt items with the lowest balances first. Of the $8.00 in the Battle Box, 50% ($4.00) is allocated to ICS, 25% ($2.00) to CD-52, 19% (1.50) to Emergency, and 6% (50¢) to War Room. Of the $5.00 in The Vault, 50% ($2.50) is allocated to the HSA, 30% ($1.50) to 401K, and 20% ($1.00) to the IRA(s). Of the $4.00 in the Builder Box, 30% ($1.20) is allocated to SWANs, 22% (88¢) to Growth, 22% (88¢) to Dividends, 13% (52¢) to Risky, 9% (36¢) to Foolish, and 4% (16¢) to Crypto. And, of the 3.00 in the Operations Box, 70% ($2.10) is allocated to Plans, and 30% (90¢) to Throw Away. Obviously, if you have more After Shave money, you can make faster progress, but remember that this is based on percentages, and the amounts actually don't matter. The Constrictor represents a 3-Month discretionary window that delivers extreme program flexibility, in regards to allocation targets.

High Interest, Revolving Debt

▶ Is a Line of Credit that remains open and usable, even if you have a balance or are paying it down.
▶ Has a preset, usable limit that is available On-Demand.
▶ Will charge you a penalty, known as interest, based on how much you have used and owe.

What matters most is actually getting started, creating a process, following a plan, gaining experience, gaining knowledge, and exhibiting consistent discipline, every day, of every week, of every year, year in and year out. You can relax, once you've hit your goals. And, I can almost guarantee that by the time you hit your goals, **the endeavor will have become the pleasure**. This system is built for poor people. If you notice in the earlier Social Security Earnings chart example, this person had averaged less than $1,000 in earnings for 6 straight years. I know this scenario is legit, because these numbers are mine (but years are different). I edited the values after 2009, for modesty's sake. Although not as sophisticated as it would become, since I didn't know enough in the late 1980s, the basic philosophy and tenets were already in place. I had already begun carving money up into distinct buckets, no matter how little I had.

Again, the ultimate goal, from the very beginning, is to gain time under tension and experience. Learn as you go, so that when you find yourself receiving large sums of money (inheritance, raises, promotions, etc.), you'll know what you're doing. Waiting to start, until you have more money, is foolish. Do it now. Win now. Achieve now. The only alteration I might make is to perhaps allocate a chunk of money to the Throw Away account, before starting, in earnest. You don't want to be sidelined by an errant night of weakness culminating with a Big Mac, Pizza Hut, Taco Bell, Coca-Cola, Little Debbie binge-fest – true story. This delicious scenario has bit me more than once.

The Anabolic Approach Explained

What You Make vs. What You Keep

The Fisicality Prime Calculations Worksheet has principle preservation, coupled with asset value appreciation, as its foundational principle. For the strength athlete, muscle tissue and/or strength preservation, coupled with muscle growth and/or strength increase is the foundational principle. The investor researches potential holdings, while also analyzing the current portfolio, for alignment. The strength athlete researches potential techniques, supplements, and routines, while also analyzing the current approach, for effectiveness. The investor and strength athlete both establish baselines that they do not want to violate, nor do they want to indulge in activities that deviate from the intended purposes of **resource preservation and growth**. Whereas the investor never wants his portfolio value to drop below the principle contribution, the strength athlete never wants their size or strength to fall below a set, established value. They both excel at deploying countermeasures and safeguards, to ensure this outcome. The investor will set entry prices for buys and automatic sell prices, for owned securities. The strength athlete will use the scale and body fat measurements, to maintain body composition targets. Or, they will use the calculator to make sure that their current higher rep workouts still align with what their projected 1-rep max would be.

For a bodybuilder preparing for a contest or a powerlifter preparing for a meet, monitoring and review become even more critical. The contest ready bodybuilder's structure can vary wildly, even with minimal changes to intake of fluids, salt, and carbohydrates. For powerlifters, a 2-inch discrepancy in hand spacing or foot spacing can impact a given lift by 20 lbs. or more. At this point the experienced investor and lifter are keenly focused on not making any unforced errors. They are in a constant execution and evaluation cycle. The OODA Loop is now second nature and is used for every aspect of their work. Although it may seem monotonous to some, these dedicated athletes find **comfort in the monotony** and the consistent improvement that they are experiencing. Essentially, they are in The Zone, and that was the unspoken desire, all along.

Money Set

___

Keep Those Gains

Some bodybuilders compete several times, each year and are able to not only maintain but grow, while losing body fat. The keys to success are intelligent planning, monitoring, and not deviating from the plan.

FORCED REPS & DROP SETS

30-60%

Of Total Body Fat Reduction

With Low to No Muscle Loss

- **Contest Prep** Bodybuilders
- **5% Body Fat** After Prep

(Bauer et al., 2023)

Accounts List

When you begin a business relationship with a company, you sign a contract, and you and the other party agree to certain terms. The difference is most companies keep track of what they signed; they archive it. They also keep track of your history with them, monitor activity, and take note of any changes and anomalies. And, if a change or anomaly gives them pause, they address it or sever the relationship. Most consumers do none of those things. They don't even read over the contracts that they sign, much less archive them. And, aside from a cursory glance, to take note of their balances and perhaps a due date, they don't track anything in the way of changes on the partner side. These are mistakes. At a minimum, every entity you do business with should have its pertinent information cataloged somewhere, in a form you can easily understand and easily access.

It's critical that you, as a consumer, start to expose yourself to the language that businesses use, even if you don't understand it. And, make no mistake, these languages are foreign languages. Doctors, lawyers, computer technicians, politicians, militaries, companies, etc. all use foreign languages. **The words may be the same, but the intent, meaning, and understanding of what is being communicated is often unintelligible to those who are not initiated into their ecosystems.** And, this ignorance is detrimental to your well-being in all aspects. A web search for "online contract reviewer" can provide you with resources to assist with your understanding the terms of an agreement. "Viral" means one thing to social media platforms, another thing to doctors, and yet something else to computer technicians. And, the implication of the word has a negative connotation, using the language of one arena, and a positive connotation, in another. But, that's a simple example. What about something like NAS, for example. In medicine, it's Neonatal Abstinence Syndrome, in the military, it's Naval Air Station, in computing it's Networked Attached Storage, and in hip-hop, it's Nasir bin Olu Dara Jones. One of the things I disdain about some of the people who are versed in some of these languages is the smugness, entitlement, and conceit they often exhibit. They intentionally make it difficult to follow conversations and understand information. This is why I typically scour PubMed, in addition to simplified learning resources, when dealing with doctors. I want to be able to speak the lingo well enough to not be taken

ACCOUNTS LIST POTENTIAL COLUMNS

Company Name	Status	Renewal Type
Category	Last Activity	Auto Renew Status
Type	Owner	Cost
Account Name	Billing Cycle	Pay Method
Account Number	Billing Method	Bundle Status
Routing Number	Renewal Cycle	Discounts

advantage of. And, I also want to understand a citizen's basic legal rights, when it comes to dealing with the police for home, travel, and public situations. I'm not picking on those two industries, but many doctors know very little about the basics of certain conditions, and many police officers know very little about the basics of some of the laws they are charged with enforcing. Educate yourself and watch the look of bewilderment on their faces, and prepare for the bullying tactics and aggressive demeanor shifts that occur, once they are challenged and exposed. However, the best-in-class of these professionals take these challenges as opportunities to learn more, educate you, and/or improve their skills. However, your failure to educate yourself on the basics of some of the most impactful elements in your life, leaves you significantly more ignorant than the doctors and police, used in the previous example. Plus, you are putting your family and its future at risk.

Trust Nothing; Believe Nothing; Verify Everything; Question Everything.

In your accounts list, you can create a column for as many attributes as you want, as well as link it to an archive location where you store downloaded documents, if you wish. At a minimum, you should try to capture any information you feel you might need, if you were attempting to resolve an issue with a business entity. Also, it's not uncommon to have a need to go back several years, or even several decades, to review information that the business didn't archive and no longer has. Sometimes, this old information just might be the thing that helps you get your Top Secret clearance, secure that home loan, remove erroneous info from your credit report, avoid jail time, or save your life.

ACCOUNTS LIST The Accounts List needs to have every account that you currently have or have had that you can remember. It is common to have a need to use information from some old account you haven't touched in years, for one thing or another. At a minimum, this resource should be divided into active and inactive account sections. Also, any account for any resource that you use should be in this list, not just bank accounts or merchants. Got an AARP membership –put it in here. Yahoo Email – put it in here. FaceSpace, TicTac, Burger Monarch accounts – put them in here. If you have a username and password for a resource, put it in the list. You never know when a problem will arise and you will need information quickly, about who you've done business with.

COLUMNS (CONT.)

Authentication	Primary Contact	Business Hours
MFA Enabled	Contact Phone	Anniversary Date
URL	Contact Email	Cancellation Status
Support Phone	PIN	Cancellation Date
Support Email	Access Number	Active Issues
Support Portal	Mailing Address	Notes

Stock Shares are Your "Employees"

I am a Value investor. I try to find well-managed, high quality companies, with a moat or business advantage, at discounted rates. I want to buy everything below market value. I don't worry about missing out on the latest hot pick that just doubled in price, in the last 30 days. Everything eventually reverts back to the mean. I'll buy it then. And, if it doesn't revert quickly, I'm OK with that, too. I'll accept my "loss", without remorse. You can't win them all, and if something has ALREADY exploded in price, **you're ALREADY too late**. When I buy a stock, I consider myself an owner of that company, in a very real way. The brick and mortal of it are notable to me. The products and services they offer are important to me. The customer interactions they engage in are significant to me. From my perspective, I'm buying a company not a security. So, when I purchase a stock, I do

Employees Needed to Generate $10,000 Annually
Sample calculations, based on data collected 08JUL2024.
(MarketWatch, 2024)

Employee (Stock)	Per Employee Salary (Price)	Per Employee Annual Cash Generated (Dividend)	Employees to Generate $10,000 Annually (Shares)	Cost to Hire Employees Generating $10,000 (Total Cost)
Realty Income	$53.09	$3.16	3,165	$168,006
Microsoft	$467.56	$3.00	3,333	$1,558,533
Ares Capital	$21.10	$1.92	5,208	$109,896
SCHD	$77.02	$2.56	3,906	$300,859

it planning to enter into a lifetime relationship. I'm not planning on selling it, unless there is an exigent circumstance, or my thesis on why I bought it changes, or it no longer aligns with my program. So, although I enter into a stock purchase for "Always and Forever", Heatwave style, as soon as it no longer aligns with what I want, I get rid of it, "Don't Think Twice", Bob Dylan style, but soaked in Con Funk Shun's, "I'm Leaving Baby" swag – suppressed emotion but no regret. I harden myself to ignore any influence by its history, past performance, logo, advertisements, ticker symbol familiarity, or anything else, for any aspect of the company, that provides me with a level of comfort derived from chumminess. Again, buy a good company, at a good price, and hold it forever, unless it violates your protocol.

One of the most important aspects of investing, at least to me, is dividends. Well, maybe not just to me. Depending on which source you follow and their logic regarding the phenomenon, reinvested, compounded dividends comprise anywhere from 30% to a whopping 90% of total stock market returns, since around the 1940s. Now, **I will never shun a low or no dividend company**. However, if all other things are equal between two companies, 80% of the time I'll choose the one that either pays a dividend, has a higher dividend, has a higher dividend growth rate, has a higher dividend safety score, etc., you get the picture; there are still lots of things to consider. Things like share issuance rate, share buybacks, LEGIT EARNINGS ON FREE CASH FLOW (FCF) REPORTING, and simple P/E are things that can quickly slow my decisioning, for a company I'm interested in. But, getting back to the dividends, my goal is to not only enjoy share price appreciation but to also capture steady, tangible returns and income. And, I

Dividend Tax Rate for 2023

Tax rates for qualified dividends, based on taxable income, for tax year 2023.
(IRS Pub. 550, 2023)

Tax Filing Status	0% Tax Rate	15% Tax Rate	20% Tax Rate
Single	$0 to $44,625	$44,626 to $492,300	$492,301 or greater
Married, Filing Jointly	$0 to $89,250	$89,251 to $553,850	$553,851 or greater
Married, Filing Separately	$0 to $44,625	$44,626 to $276,900	$276,901 or greater
Head of Household	$0 to $59,750	$59,751 to $523,050	$523,051 or greater

believe dividends are one of the best ways to do that. I view every stock share that I purchase as an Employee for The Hodge Company, Incorporated, LLC, DBA, Enterprises. And, each one of those Employees **makes** me a certain amount of money. And, each one of those Employees **costs** me a certain amount of money, to put them to work for me; I have to invest in them to get them going. The price I pay for each Employee is rarely the same, even from the same source, depending on when I bought them. This means they all have different yield-on-cost values. But, that's OK, as I simply need my cost to fall within an acceptable, value range. Now, once I have some Workers, I can count on a certain amount of productivity from them, if dividends are involved. This essentially means, I can determine how many Employees I need to hit an income target, and I know definitively how much I need to invest to hit that target.

Stock Shares are Your "Employees", Continued

For example, in an August of 2024 scenario, if I use Realty Income (O) which costs $60.16 per share, pays a currently monthly dividend of $0.26 per share, and has a 5-year average dividend growth rate of 3.55%, I'll need 3,165 shares at a cost of $190,380 in order to generate $10,000 in annual income. If I want to generate the average 2023 U.S. wage of $65,470, I'll need 20,718 shares at a cost of $1,246,416. But, wait. What if I use a stock that pays a higher dividend? If I go with Ares Capital (ARCC) which costs $20.57 per share, pays a calculated monthly dividend of $0.16 per share, and has a 5-year dividend annual growth rate of 3.97%, I need 34,099 shares at a cost of $701,416, to generate that same $65,470 annually. That's 44% less in cash outlay for the same result. Additionally, both of these stocks have dividend growth rates that should match or outpace inflation in any given year, based on the Federal Reserve's reported 30-year average inflation rate of 2.13%. But, as always, there are

> **When You Can't See The Forest For The Trees Or The Trees For The Leaves, stick to the simpler structures. These more complex models require vision and macroviewing capability.**

other considerations, such as, volatility, dependability, consistency, core asset price appreciation, asset quality, etc. But, the bottom line here is, if I create a portfolio of dividend stocks, distribute the load in a sensible manner that provides safety and solid returns, I can easily calculate my point-in-time costs to hit an annual target payout. This means, all of my Workers can pay all of my living expenses, moving forward. Also, if this is my only income, and I can live beneath my means, I can continue to devote a portion of those dividends towards future purchases to add even more Employees, every single month, supercharging my annualized payout growth rate. If for some reason I decided to not use any dividend money for expenses, but instead reinvested it all to buy more Workers, after 1 year I would have:

Realty Income - 1048 more shares, raises total annual income to $70,845
Assumes 3% annual dividend growth and 3.8% annual price appreciation
Ares Capital - 3111 more shares, raises total annual income to $73,587
Assumes 3% annual dividend growth and 2.3% annual price appreciation

This means that my annual share count (Employees) and dividend payout (Salary) would begin to increase exponentially, as each year's increase would subsequently increase the next year's buying power. Also, the tax rate for qualified dividend income is different than that of ordinary dividends or earned income. Qualified dividends are taxed as capital gains. The dividend tax rate is 0% for the first $44,465 for a single person and 0% for the first $89,250 for a married couple filing jointly, as of 2024 – **That's $89,250 Tax Free!** After that, the tax rate for the next $187,650 is only 15%, for a married couple filing jointly. With all of these relatively safe tools at our disposal, I'm always mystified when I see the famous, rich athletes, lottery winners, trust funds babies, movie stars, etc. go broke. I mean, if someone had $5,000,000 to spend (which some people have, as a portion of their wealth), the conservative vehicle of Realty Income would generate an initial $262,633 in annual income. And, it can do this with no other input, no additional money, no management, and no anything else — nothing else, at all. It can do all of this, simply by someone just owning the stock. Keeping all of the inputs static, after 5 years the annual income would be $388,266. And, after 10 years, the annual income balloons up to $568,846. And again, the kicker for all of this is, as dividend income, this money comes in without your working, with no further input on your part, 24 hours a day, 7 days a week - no matter what you're doing. Eating a sandwich — you're making money. Watching cartoons — you're still making money. Working out at the gym - yup, making money. Sleeping late — bagging moolah. **I wish I had found the book I'm writing right now, when I was 12-years-old**. This would have been the easiest decision in the world for me to make, even then.

Now, with all of that said, I would be amiss, if I didn't also relay to you my perspective and approach regarding the other Builder Box categories, with an emphasis on the riskier categories. Don't make the mistake and think for a second that just because I'm intrinsically and purposefully a Value investor, that I don't exploit opportunities with riskier assets, because I do. To be a well-rounded and thoughtful investor, I also indulge in riskier assets, as a rule. However, I have a strict system and what I feel are intelligent, safety protocols that are in place and adhered to, for this activity. **Risk is not something to take on haphazardly, but taking it is a must.**

The following quote is one of my favorites and has been somewhat of a guiding mantra, for several years, for me. Unfortunately, I can't find this quote, in any of the many copies and translations of Machiavelli's "The Prince", that I've studied. I see this quote quite often, but I don't know what all of the other authors are using for their actual source (book and page number(s)), and I question their thoroughness. It may simply be a clever paraphrase, but even then, I'd still like to credit its originator. Regardless, I consider it an excellent sentiment, and I include it here.

ALL COURSES OF ACTION ARE RISKY. SO, PRUDENCE IS NOT IN AVOIDING DANGER (THAT'S IMPOSSIBLE), BUT IN CALCULATING RISK AND ACTING DECISIVELY. MAKE MISTAKES OF AMBITION AND NOT MISTAKES OF SLOTH. DEVELOP THE STRENGTH TO TAKE BOLD ACTION AND NOT THE STRENGTH TO SUFFER.

— ATTRIBUTED TO NICCOLÒ MACHIAVELLI
(Machiavelli, 1513/1981)

FISICALITY

SECTION 6

LANDING

Cycles Analyses and Refinements

The 12-Month Cycle is designed to ensure 75% focus on the All Debt Payoff, if it is the active PRIME. If ADP is not the active PRIME, a lesser focus on the various Second Level PRIMEs is activated.

1 - JAN
9-Month PRIME Cycle Begins

2 - FEB
Maintain Protocols

3 - MAR
Maintain Protocols

4 - APR
Analysis & Adjustments

12 - DEC
3-Month Cycle Ends & 12-Month Cycle Planning

5 - MAY
Maintain Protocols

The 9-Month Cycle within the 12-Month Core Cycle is actually 3 cycles of 3-months each. At the end of each cycle, adjustments are made, based on progress during that sub-cycle. The objective after each sub-cycle is to reassess progress in tracking towards satisfying the PRIME, accounting for any changes to the landscape.

11 - NOV
Maintain Protocols

6 - JUN
Maintain Protocols

10 - OCT
3-Month Constrictor Window Begins

9 - SEP
9-Month PRIME Target Ends

8 - AUG
Maintain Protocols

7 - JUL
Analysis & Adjustments

The 3-Month Constrictor Window that takes place, during the last 3-month cycle, provides program flexibility. You can continue with the scheduled plan, revert to an earlier step in the plan, or develop an entirely new protocol, for the next 3 months. However, regardless of what is implemented here, the Next Regular Cycle's PRIME Structure is implemented, as scheduled and on time.

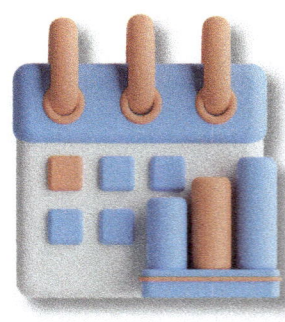

Working and Building with the PRIMEs

To reiterate, your PRIME is the main category you want to focus on. It is your priority. The PRIME categories in this book are: All Debt Payoff, Battle Box, The Vault, Builder Box, and Operations Box, but you can create your own. Then, inside of each PRIME, the elements inside of it are ranked. The key concept to grasp is only one category can function as the active PRIME, at any given time. If ADP is the active PRIME, all other PRIMEs are deactivated. This doesn't mean that the other PRIME categories are ignored, though. They are still managed and still have regular, active transactions. They simply have a smaller amount of the available funds allocated to them, as the bulk of the money is reserved for the ACTIVE PRIME. However, once the current active PRIME's cycle is finished or it's targets are satisfied, it is deactivated and the next PRIME in the hierarchy is marked as active. Walking through the calendar example, let's assume that the ADP PRIME is active. We start with it in JAN. And by start, I mean that we allocate funds to all of the accounts, using the money from the Razor's After Shave. Recall that the After Shave is all of the money that remains, after all operational and bare minimum obligations have been satisfied. We allocate funds according to the ADP schedule, in JAN, and verify that all transactions are valid and complete, as planned. We make sure to pay attention, so that the amounts agree with what we have planned and that everything is processed on time, with no NSF, returns, or misses. This continues for FEB and MAR; we're just executing, at this point. APR marks the end of the first 3-Month, mini cycle and the beginning of the next mini cycle. In APR, we assess our performance during the last cycle, and make any necessary adjustments, if we find there are complications with payments, accounts, or relationships with vendors. Once this analysis is finished, we continue executing, until the beginning of the next mini cycle, in JUL. We repeat the analysis and adjustments as necessary and continue executing, until the beginning of the next mini cycle, in OCT. This mini cycle deviates from the previous three, as it is the Constrictor Window. Here we perform an assessment and make a determination, for where we want to concentrate our funds, for the next 3 months. We can continue with the current active PRIME, or we can choose another PRIME. Or, we can even divert funds to a passion project or some other thing that is important to us. But, we can only do it, for this last mini cycle. We must reengage with the regular PRIME at the beginning of the next full cycle. Then, the whole process starts again, continuing in perpetuity.

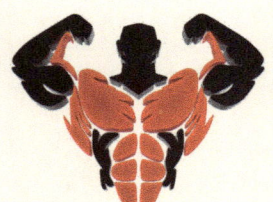

The Anabolic Approach Explained

Leveling Up

By using a cyclical approach to training, the lifter establishes definitive points-in-time to refer to and use as baselines for subsequent work. The end of a training cycle delineates completion. If it was a good cycle, you get to preserve it in stone and can always refer back to that time and feel proud of what you accomplished. This can be very inspiring, when beginning another cycle. If it was a subpar cycle, you get to close the book on it, file it away, and shrug off the baggage associated with it. This allows you to keep the Lessons Learned while isolating any negatives that could hamper future cycles' effectiveness.

This approach is also important for the investor. Take the Lessons Learned from any mistakes, but don't dwell on the losses; that money is gone, and it can only now help you, as an **experiential or analytical artifact**. In both cases, you get a clean slate. You are starting another Loop. Tooling, environments, and situations will be similar, but they will not be identical. Just because something occurred a certain way in the past does not mean it will occur in that same way moving forward. The Reality that exists for each grain of Time's falling sand is unique. It may not seem like it to us, but our entire world is completely different, at a molecular level, for every moment that passes. This means, all a person can hope for is to **make the best decision**, with the current information they have and the experience they have gained, while understanding that nothing is guaranteed, and that, cosmically speaking, at a molecular level, **each new second is a brand new, never before seen Reality**.

There is no consensus on the levels of progression required, for fiscal or physical endeavors, but I have synthesized a model from several competing models. The basics are: the Beginner knows little to nothing; the Novice may have some theoretical knowledge and/or limited practical application experience; the Intermediate has experience with success, failure, and normalcy and knows how to navigate within a given ecosystem; the Advanced have mastered all competency skills; and the Expert has mastered all of the competency skills, along with the discipline's theories, and has perfected utilizing unconventional methods, in process.

Money Set

_____
_____
_____
_____
_____
_____
_____
_____
_____
_____
_____

Hodgerian Fisicality Progression Levels

Beginner	Novice	Intermediate	Advanced	Expert
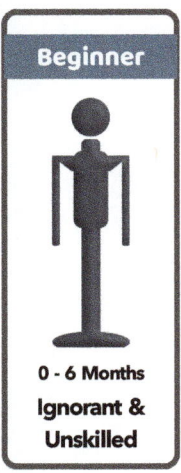				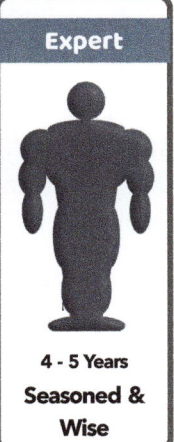
0 - 6 Months	6 - 18 Months	18 - 36 Months	3 - 4 Years	4 - 5 Years
Ignorant & Unskilled	Learning & Advancing	Competent & Capable	Proficient & Knowledgeable	Seasoned & Wise

The Mock POAM

POAM stands for Plan of Action and Milestones. A POAM is a cybersecurity document that identifies a system weakness, details the steps and resources needed to address the weakness, and tracks the status and progress towards resolution, based on a given target date. For our financial planning purposes here, we will use a mock POAM that will help us identify risks, obstacles, and required resources, as well as provide a macroview of effort. Information required includes: Item, Status, Start Date, Projected End Date, Dated Milestones, Resources Needed, Risks, and Obstacles. The POAM:

▶ Adds Refinement and Clarity of Purpose
▶ Acts as a Supplemental Tracking Mechanism for the Fisicality Worksheet
▶ Acts as a Functional Resource for Goal Setting, Objective Generation, and Tactics
▶ Aids in Analysis & Adjustments within the 12-Month Core Cycle

The POAM should be updated, as milestones are met and whenever additions, subtractions, or modifications need to be made. For my purposes, a quick review once a week is usually all I need. And, when I say quick, I mean quick. It takes me all of 5 minutes to review and update, in most cases. However, when you first start in earnest managing your money, you may find that you are looking at it several times a week for hours at a time, as you familiarize yourself with the ebbs and flows of Money Management. As a rule, I recommend conducting a review and update, at least once a week.

Sample Mock POAM

ITEM	STATUS	MILESTONE
ADP	CC Veesahhh	On Track	Payoff $1,500 Balance
ADP	CC MiserCharge	On Track	Cut $4,000 Balance to $3,500
ADP	CC Dibbards	On Track	Payoff $2,000 Balance
Battle Box	ICS	Done	Hit $500 Balance Target
Battle Box	CD-52	On Track	Create All 52 Accounts Minimum $5 Balance
Battle Box	Emergency	Degraded	Hit $1,000 Balance Target
Battle Box	War Room	Not Started	Hit $2,000 Balance Target
Vault	HSA	On Track	Contribute $8,300 Family Maximum
Vault	401K	On Track	Contribute Company Match + $12,000
Vault	IRA	Not Started	Hit 50 and Older $7,500 Maximum
Plans	Moving Expenses	On Hold	Hit $3,000 Target	Move Pending Decision
Plans	New Washer & Dryer	Degraded	Hit $2,000 Target
Builder Box	Dividend	Not Started	$1,500 Cost to Generate $10 Monthly with ARCC Stock

POAM Columns Clarified

Feel free to add or subtract columns, as needed for your purposes. For example, some may find a column for notes or a separate column for the planned date helpful. But, a basic structure includes the columns below.

ITEM
Describes the goal and objective. In the first line of the example "ADP: Credit Card Payoff", ADP (All Debt Payoff) is the Goal and Credit Card Payoff is the Objective.

STATUS
Reflects the current state of the line item. Options are: Not Started, On Track, On Hold, Degraded, and Done.

MILESTONE
Describes the individual accomplishment, criterion, or achievement, for satisfying the Objective.

START
The planned start date is identified by a trailing "- P". The actual start date is entered as a standard date. Here, the "-P" can be eliminated and replaced with color coding, such as making the planned date red, while leaving the actual date black.

END
The planned end date is identified by a trailing "- P". The actual end date is entered as a standard date. As with START above, the "-P" can be eliminated and replaced with color coding, such as making the planned date red and leaving the actual date black.

REQUIREMENTS
Describes resources or circumstances needed to satisfy achieving the MILESTONE.

OBSTACLES
Describes existing challenges in achieving the OBJECTIVE.

RISKS
Describes potential challenges in achieving the OBJECTIVE.

START	END	REQUIREMENTS	OBSTACLES	RISKS
01JAN2030	01APR2030 - P	Set as category PRIME	None	Unforeseen Charges
01AUG2030 - P	01FEB2031 - P	0	None	None
01APR2030 - P	01AUG2030 - P	Stop Using This Card	None	None
01JAN2030	01FEB2030	Overtime at Work	Work Scheduling	None
01JAN2030	31DEC2030	0	None	Forget Weekly Buy
01JUL2030	01DEC2030	0	None	None
0	0	0	None	None
15MAR2030	01AUG2030	0	None	None
15MAR2030	01AUG2030	Fund HSA & 401K First	None	None
0	0	Fund Before Deadline	None	Miss Federal Deadline
01JUN2029	01MAY2030	Finalize Decision	None	Unknown Costs
01OCT2029	01FEB2030	0	None	None
0	0	0	Market Timing	None

The Anabolic Approach Explained

Beware of Noisy Cricket Syndrome

Creating an intentional activity cycle, while also being aware of naturally occurring cycles, and how they overlap, will aid in determining their collective impact. For example, in the investment world, things like periodic earnings reports, dividend distributions, and tax-loss harvesting deadlines should align with your buy, sell, and portfolio rebalance timing. On the Anabolic side, things like school sessions, calendar seasons, and holidays should align with your optimum workout time, bulking cycle, and cutting cycle. Sometimes, you will not have the luxury of creating the most harmonious timing mix. And, sometimes, everything on your schedule will outright violently clash. Ultimately, though, if your scheduling efforts result in an immovable object meeting an irresistible force, just know that **you will suffer**. In those cases, it's just a matter of dropping your head, bracing your back, stiffening your resolve, and trudging through. Here, it is essential to create a hierarchy, consisting of the most important and impactful things, giving them priority, but not amateurishly overlooking the seemingly trivial.

Please note that a distinction needs to be made between things that are important and things that are impactful. You can easily make an error by overlooking something that is seemingly insignificant and not important to you, disregard it, and then suffer major setbacks from doing so; it actually had a significant impact, after all. Like the "Men in Black" Noisy Cricket – **don't let the smooth taste fool you**.

Strength athletes are notoriously deliberate, when it comes to developing and maintaining short-term cycles and long-term schedules. It all starts with goal setting and defining a target, such as a contest date or deadline for hitting a personal record. From there, the schedule is built around hitting whatever goal was set. Although goals tied to a specific event rarely have the latitude for adjusting targets and/or preparation for them, personal goals will provide some flexibility. Even so, most driven athletes rarely make unnecessary changes, and they treat all target dates as immutable, unless there is an emergency or an injury. And even then, they will often quickly transition back to their schedule, once the initial immediacy of any emergency has passed.

Money Set

_____
_____
_____
_____
_____
_____
_____
_____
_____
_____
_____

Hydrate Accounts

Once you have finalized your plan, it's time to create the accounts, for all of the necessary resources. Take your time here, and make sure you understand the rules, for whatever platform you are using. Banking has some particular rules with certain types of accounts, such as HSA, CD, IRA, and 401K accounts. Although you will certainly need to create bank accounts, you will also need to create access accounts with any merchant or entity you are doing business with, if they have a provision for it. This means your electric bill, gas bill, insurance bill, furniture bill, etc. should all tie back to a vendor account where you can access your records online. This is important, so that when it comes time for you to process payments, you can verify and validate the obligation info in process, directly with the vendor. I tend to open up every scheduled payment's vendor website and verify amounts, in succession, with what I have on the spreadsheet.

IDENTIFY Use your Master Accounts List spreadsheet, as the authoritative source for tracking, to ensure you create all necessary accounts.

PREPARE Gather all data, resources, and information you may need. This may include old addresses, old phone numbers, a photocopy of your driver's license, etc.

ORDER Start with the accounts you believe to be the easiest to setup. Additionally, there may be some accounts that rely on other accounts, to complete their enrollment.

PATIENCE Understand that you may run into difficulty, due to bad data, technical issues, red tape, administrative roadblocks, etc. Be patient and resilient. Some vendors may require you to mail hard copies, instead of online submissions. If so, do it.

VER/VAL Verify and Validate access, functionality, features, and account data, for each account. Make sure your name, address, etc. are all correct. Setup linked accounts and test data and/or money transfers, with small amounts, where applicable.

Archive the Data

On-Site Archive

This is the Authoritative Data for all of your resources. This archive should be updated anytime changes are made. The Fisicality Worksheet is the item that will require the most effort, with updates occurring after each bill paying cycle.

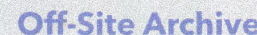

Off-Site Archive

This is the Back-Up Archive. This archive must be updated if there are credential or authentication changes. Otherwise, changes occur more infrequently here, monthly to every other month.

Now that you have gathered the data, finalized the plan, and hydrated the accounts, it's time to do a full archive of all resources. Again, even though you may have a main archive method, here I would recommend having both an analogue and digital copy of everything. So, if you are writing everything down by hand, scan everything into a digital record for storage. And, if you have everything digitized, print everything out as a hard copy for storage. Then, secure it all, very well. Physical copies need to be physically secured in a safe, lockbox, or other hardened location, and then obfuscated. Digital resources need to be encrypted, password protected, and shored up with an MFA mechanism. My current suggestion is to explore options regarding hardware security keys. If you do get a hardware security key, keep in mind that you will need two, one for use as a primary and the other as a backup, in case the primary is lost, damaged, or no longer works.

Adhere to Activity Schedule

OK. You've spent the time, put in the work, and built out the system. The only thing left now is to do everything you've planned, according to plan. Don't think about it (you've already done that), just commit, take the final action, and do it. Starting off, you should review your main spreadsheet daily, for the first 3-month cycle, even if it's only for 5 minutes, each day. As you become more sophisticated, start to research companies, buy securities, double check your work, and review data, you'll start to notice patterns and trends. Also, you'll find yourself engaging in little dollops of research to solve problems or answer questions about your activity – **as you learn more, you'll find that you need to learn more**. The bottom line here is to maintain discipline and conduct all activity, as scheduled and on time.

At this stage, the most important thing is to take action and maintain action. Too often, people just like you have ideas, good ideas, that could enrich lives. Sometimes, these ideas have been meandering around your myriad thoughts for years, popping up during the half time show of the game you're kinda sorta watching, or wedging their way in, during the blind date you should have skipped, or slowly misting up in the trails of another thought, on a lazy day, filled with piddling about. Then, sometimes, seemingly suddenly, the thoughts that were once puny trivialities have gained mass and are taking up more psychic space. But, it isn't sudden. These thoughts have been percolating for years. A plan develops. It comes together, effortlessly. It almost seems to build itself. You find yourself, simultaneously, the creator and a spectator of the process. And, this all makes sense, because as I've already mentioned, the particles of these ideas have been floating around for years, but now something has catalyzed them into forming a cohesive structure.

So, you've got an idea, and you've got a plan. The next step is to take action. And, sadly, this is where it stops, for most people, most of the time. If you really think about it, though, **the hardest part of getting started with ANYTHING is getting started with SOMETHING.** Taking meaningful action can be a far reach. You start thinking of all of the reasons why you shouldn't actually DO anything: it'll cost too much; it'll take too much time; my friends will joke me; we've got a baby on the way; I'll do it when I have more money; it will be stressful; I will fail; I don't know where to begin; I'm not smart enough; and on, and on, and on. For each of those there are counterarguments: it'll cost you more, if you don't try; time isn't something you have, it's something you take; joking you and not supporting you are two different things; the baby will be proud of you, for taking a chance, when they've grow up; you'll never have enough money to do anything that you're scared to do; suck it up, buttercup; you might not achieve your goal, but you only fail, if you don't try; begin from wherever you are; **if you're not smart enough that's good, as you won't be aware of the mistakes you're making that would make a smarter person quit,** before they achieve success. It doesn't matter what the argument is; there is a counter to it. Just get started. Just start splashing about, even if you don't fully know what you're doing. And, before you know it, you'll find that you've made steps away from where you were. If some of those steps were in the wrong direction, you now have a modest bit of experience to know you're going the wrong way and that you need to change course. **You can do it.**

Rich People Have Small T.V.s and Big Libraries, and Poor People Have Small Libraries and Big T.V.s.

– Zig Zieglar

RULES OF ENGAGEMENT

Stick to the Plan
You have built the plan, so stick to it. Become an organic machine, void of emotion. The only thing that matters now is executing, regardless of the short-term impact.

Maintain Discipline
Do not allow yourself to become weak-minded. True discipline is an internal trait. It does not exist outside of the Self. Be willing to suffer, to achieve your Goals.

Don't Get Impatient
Control your desire to see massive changes in short time frames. Remember, you are trying to establish a new pattern, a new Way of living.

Don't Second Guess
You have built-in, periodic, analysis points. Use them. Unless there is an exigency, major changes should wait, until the next quarterly review.

The Anabolic Approach Explained

Add a Little Bit, All the Time

The strength athlete toils away week in and week out, making modest gains, if things are going well, but incurring losses, if things are going not going well. For the Fisicality CD-52 plan, a meager bit of money is added to an individual CD, every Friday, of every week, of every year. For the strength athlete who is committed, a meager amount of weight may be added each week, for many exercises throughout the year. Mr. Olympia winners, Phil Heath and Dorian Yates, famously had workout routines that resulted in each body part receiving direct work, one day a week. Ronnie Coleman, another dominant Mr. Olympia winner, reportedly had a workout split that hit each body part, twice each week.

Regardless of whether a split hits each body part once per week or twice per week, you have a **known value** to work with. Let's say we use the once per week split, and we realistically assert that 4 weeks will be Off weeks, due to vacations, breaks, recoveries, de-loading, and such. Also, cutting cycles, Unplanned Aways, illnesses, business travel, etc. may cut into pure growth phases, so we can conservatively subtract another 12 weeks. This results in us having 36 pure growth workouts, per body part. But, let's be excessive and use Yates' and Heaths' 1x a week per body part, every week, for every year, with no breaks. This gives us 52 workouts a year.

If we use the chest workout, as an example that follows the CD-52 Method of adding meager amounts of a thing each cycle, for each workout where meager increases are made, what is the impact? What happens if an Intermediate lifter adds, say an average of 1 1/2 lbs. to their current 315 lb. x 8 rep bench press every workout? At the end of the year, they would theoretically be benching 393 lbs., for at least a single. Powerlifters know the secret of using **little bitty plates** to get massive gains, without their incurring injury or dipping too far into their ability to recover. I've even heard of some powerlifters using 1/2 pound, magnetic plates to make consistent gains. So, whether we are talking about Money Matters or Anabolic Endeavors, consistently making small additions to the things you are already doing, can yield major benefits and pay increased dividends.

Money Set

_____

_____

_____

_____

_____

_____

_____

_____

_____

_____

_____

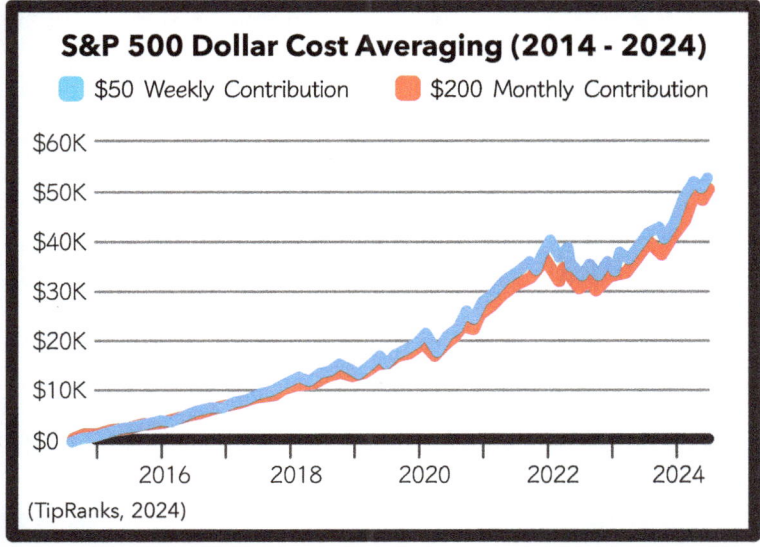

S&P 500 Dollar Cost Averaging (2014 - 2024)

🔵 $50 _Weekly Contribution_   🟠 $200 _Monthly Contribution_

(TipRanks, 2024)

Comparable DCA Results

Over this 10-year period, portfolio final values are $53,586 for weekly, and $50,303, for monthly. I prefer the frequency of the weekly contribution.

Monitoring and Adjustments

Verify that everything remains on schedule, as you originally planned it, and ensure that you are thoroughly monitoring your activity. This may be as simple as making sure that you double check your scheduled payments list, after you set them up, or that you check your Bill Payer account, after a few days, to make sure all payments were successful. I have on occasion made errors by doubling up on a payment, or paying the wrong amount for an item, or skipping an item, altogether. Double, triple, and quadruple checking are second nature to me, and mistakes are rare, but they still happen. Sometimes, things outside our control happen, and we are forced to make concessions. If you are still in the early stages, you may not have the ICS or Emergency fund targets populated, to handle happenstance. That's OK. Do what you have to do to solve the issue(s) at hand, and immediately get back on track.

The Importance of Monitoring

Remember when you got that 3-speed, banana-seat Huffy, with the high-rise, chopper handlebars. Tooling around the back roads on that thing, you had to pay attention to the terrain, any traffic that might popup, every weird bike sound or sensation that wasn't there before, the weather, dogs, snakes, and pretty much everything else. But, you always seemed to make it back home safe and mostly sound. And, regardless of how often you rode and how effortless (and even mundane) some of your rides were, you always remained dependent on gathering information, during the ride, and making adjustments, as needed. Learning how to effectively monitor is critical to success in most endeavors. You will be constantly bombarded with

Reasons to Monitor

Although I'm using the term Monitor, I'm using it with the understanding that it encompasses Environment Monitoring, Data Capture, and Information Analysis. This is the triumvirate that will most significantly impact your decision-making.

- ▶ Reveal Anomalies
- ▶ Increase Planning Effectiveness
- ▶ Establish the Best Data to Capture
- ▶ Establish the Best Information to Analyze
- ▶ Decisioning that Yields Desired Results
- ▶ Accurately Forecast Possible Outcomes
- ▶ Reduce Situational Anxiety
- ▶ Create Baseline for What is Normal

information, when working on a thing. It's up to you to determine what data are information, for your purposes. And, as in the bike-riding example above, you will then need to determine what adjustments, if any, need to made, based on that information. But, it all starts with the monitoring. As far as captured resources go, there is nothing more important than the data; they rank just beneath Time and the fiscal Principle (Seed Money).

The Credit Score Revisited

As you conduct your work, you will become very familiar with your credit report and its subsequent credit score. You'll know what's on the credit report, and you'll know where your credit score typically ranges, so if a sudden, drastic change occurs, you'll be poised to investigate it. But, what does your score mean, and how can it impact you. Most lenders use 5 Score ranges to place borrowers: Deep Subprime, Subprime, Near-Prime, Prime, and Super-Prime. Where your score falls can significantly impact your options and terms when it

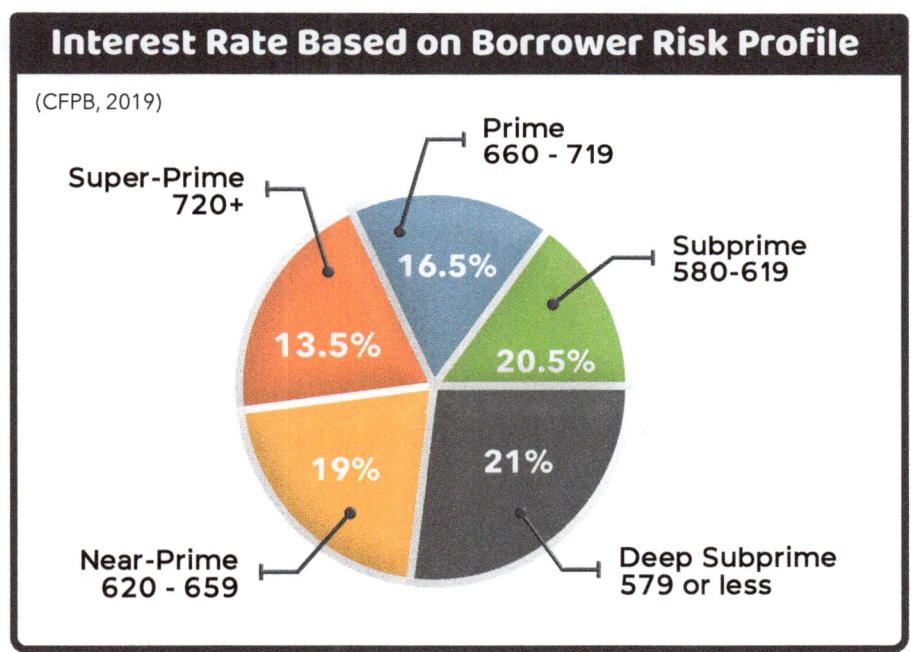

Interest Rate Based on Borrower Risk Profile

(CFPB, 2019)

- Super-Prime 720+ — 13.5%
- Prime 660 - 719 — 16.5%
- Subprime 580-619 — 20.5%
- Deep Subprime 579 or less — 21%
- Near-Prime 620 - 659 — 19%

comes to borrowing money. Generally speaking, most bankers consider Prime scores and above good scores, and people in those ranges typically enjoy favorable terms. However, people that fall into the lower Prime classifications will suffer via higher interest rates, higher fees, higher down payment requirements, and smaller loan amount limits. Additionally, **predatory loans** like Payday Loans, Subprime Mortgages, and Title Loans, are usually not a good idea, except for the most dire circumstances. If nothing with your situation is going to fundamentally change within 30 - 60 days of getting that loan, it would be wise to consider skipping it. In that scenario, after 60 days, you will be in essentially the exact same place, except now you have put your collateral at risk, paid for add-ons and fees you didn't understand, and have a new **triple-digit interest rate** from the last loan that rolled over, which sports another end-of-term balloon payment. To remix the wisdom of **DJ Quik**:

If It Doesn't Make Dollars, It Doesn't Make Sense.

The Anabolic Approach Explained

Tracking and Adjustments

Anna Bolick, Diana Ball, and Trent Bologna were preparing for a fitness contest. One week from the contest date, Anna discovered that she was 5 pounds heavier than scheduled. Over the next week, she ended up ramping up her fat loss efforts, beyond what was planned. This resulted in her coming into the contest, not at her best, somewhat depleted, and flat. Diana, on the other hand, meticulously tracked her progress each day and noticed a pattern of being ½ pound overweight for several days in a row, at the 6-week out mark. Because of this, she made **timely minor adjustments** and continued to track progress and make additional changes, as needed. This allowed her to nail her conditioning and compete with her best package ever. Trent was a mass monster and didn't care about being shredded. He just wanted to be the mostest, hugest, biggest guy on stage, which he was. His plan resulted in his being lean but not completely diced and peeled, and he was fine with that.

There is a sweet spot for tracking that is optimal, for whatever the goal is, and most strength athletes do employ some form of tracking mechanism. Too little tracking can result in unwanted surprises. Too much tracking can result in high anxiety and false flags. The lifter in a bulking phase who is trying to gain 15 lbs. over 3 months probably doesn't need to check their weight more than a few times each week (even though I know they are going to still check it every day). Conversely, Anna should have probably been checking her weight multiple times a day, as she got closer to the contest date. It is important to remember that there will always be fluctuations up or down when tracking progress. However, the **general trend** that you see should smoothly flow, in your desired direction.

Similarly, in the finance world, stock performance will ebb and flow, sometimes drastically, but the basic trend should be in your desired direction. The thing that separates the poor investor from the adept investor and the flat, undefined competitor from the full bodied and chiseled competitor is not just how well they interpret the tracked data but also how well they make impactful, positive adjustments from them.

Money Set

_____

_____

_____

_____

_____

_____

_____

_____

_____

_____

_____

The Worm

Dennis Rodman, nicknamed "The Worm", was a forward in the NBA. The defensive and rebound specialist was known to habitually lift weights, before games, and heavier weights, AFTER games.

FORCED REPS & DROP SETS

(Rodman, 1996)

Battle Beast

Rodman was frequently assigned the toughest player to guard, on opposing teams, and he would shut them down. Of the Top 100 highest, single game, rebound performances, Dennis Rodman has 21 of them, with his highest total being 34. The next closet player has 7.

(Dhariwal, 2022)

Full Cycle Assessment

The Constrictor Window is where you "SQUEEZE" every bit of performance out of your money. The only thing you need to do here is determine if it's prudent to use the 3-Month Constrictor Window as designed, by choosing an area of focus that deviates from the current PRIME, or if you need to maintain the structure you used for the previous, 9-Month period. If everything is on track, move to the 3-Month Constrictor Window, as it's designed. This will provide some variability and freshness, along with giving you the new motivation associated with working on something you're excited about. Try to choose a focus area that exists in your Top 3 Want-To-Dos. Now, if this Want-To-Do happens to be part of an existing PRIME, that's even better, but it doesn't have to be. Be mindful that, after the Constrictor Window ends, it's back to focused work on the PRIME.

Key Assessment Metrics

1

OBJECTIVES NOT MET
If all planned objectives were not met, use the Constrictor Window to satisfy them. Any time that remains, after doing so, can be used as you see fit. For example, if you are able to satisfy any missed 9-Month Cycle objectives, during the first 30 days of the Constrictor Window, you'd still have 60 days of discretionary Constrictor Window time, available to use.

2

OBJECTIVES MET
Were all of the objectives satisfied, as planned? If so, you have the flexibility to redirect funds, as your imagination sees fit, during the 3-Month Constrictor Window.

3

PROJECTIONS
Make rough projections to determine the 3-Month outcome, if you were to maintain course or if you were to deviate from it. This will be helpful in determining the appropriate Constrictor Window course of action.

4

WANT AND DESIRE
Determine the one item that would give you the most pleasure to work towards. This is a viable option, if the 9-Month Cycle was successful.

DON'T OVERTHINK

As you go through the Assessment, don't worry about trying to get everything perfect. Do your best for each piece and quickly move on. You can revisit and refine, later. The idea here is to constantly improve by having frequent iterations that allow you to improve, enhance, and refine.

LESSONS LEARNED

Do your best to capture a bulletized brief of the things you've learned, your misconceptions, and the surprise revelations that occurred over the last cycle. You'll probably have a couple of I'm-Not-Going-To-Do-That-Again items. Over time, you'll notice that the occurrence of errors will drop and then level off. And, no matter how hard you try, those errors will stay within a certain range. This is to be expected, as it shows that you are constantly learning and growing, while also becoming increasingly proficient at fiscal administration. It is not uncommon to explore more sophisticated tools and techniques, as your body of knowledge increases. The objective of Lessons Learned is to introduce meaningful changes that improve procedures and behavior.

Tips to Improve Your Review

Create a checklist of every management resource that you regularly use. Make a determination on its effectiveness, what can be improved, if it can be replaced or consolidated, and how critical it is to your success. Trim the fat.

Some Areas of Interest

▶ The Tracking Mechanism Itself
▶ Resources In the Fisicality Worksheet
▶ Archive Solution(s)
▶ Password Manager
▶ Security, Backup, and Archive Processes
▶ Monthly Administration Procedures
▶ And Everything Else, Regularly Used

Perform a Sanity Check

Perform a self-assessment of your mentality towards the project. Focus on how energized and motivated you are or aren't. Take note of the times where your discipline slipped. Also, take note of how fast you were able to rebound after setbacks.

WHO IS DOMINANT?

▶ **THE ID**

▶ **THE EGO**

▶ **THE SUPEREGO**

Freud's Psychic Apparatus

Introduced in 1923's "The Ego and the Id ", Sigmund Freud's theoretical, psychological, structural model consists of 3 interlaced elements within the human psyche: The Id, The Ego, and The Superego.
(Freud, 1922)

APPARATUS ELEMENTS

▶ **The Id**
• Present at Birth
• Controlled by Pleasure Principle
• Comprised of Eros & Thanatos
• Eros is Pleasure Instinct
• Thanatos is Destruction Instinct
• Manifests Between Ages 0-2

▶ **The Ego**
• Not Present at Birth
• Develops from Id Experiences
• Mediator for Id & Superego
• Manifests Between Ages 2-4

▶ **The Superego**
• Not Present at Birth
• Maintains Values & Morals
• Invokes the Ideal Self
• Manifests Between Ages 4-5

Conduct Next Cycle's Preflight

This final step is actually the first step, for the next cycle. As with the last cycle, all of the real brain power and decisioning happens here. In all of the other steps, the assessments were cursory and designed only to keep you on track or resolve tactical situations. The decisions made here are global, thorough, and strategic. It is critical that we don't disregard or overlook some element, consideration, calculation, or formula. Slow down on this work, if you have the luxury. If not, go as fast as you can but not faster than you're capable. Essentially, we are simply following the OODA Loop, a tactical tool used in a strategic way. We can map the steps below as:

1. **Evaluation** ➔ **O**bserve
2. **Objectives** ➔ **O**rient
3. **Finalize** ➔ **D**ecide
4. **Execute** ➔ **A**ct

START

1

EVALUATION - Review the final results of the 9-Month and 3-Month Cycles. Establish data driven determinations on the effectiveness of the last plan and its elements.

2

OBJECTIVES - Establish new objectives, based on the Assessment results and calculate projections that provide target delivery dates and their balances.

3

FINALIZE - Create the POAM, specifying final objectives, dated milestones, resources needed, and risks. Populate the Fisicality Worksheet elements with the target data. Update all remaining Fisicality Worksheet elements.

4

EXECUTE - This is the second time through and will be less complex. Get to work, and get to it. Don't think about it. Just do it (incidental rhyme).

END

Penthouse |⸺

A good boxer attacks, with Bunches of Punches, from the top **(Penthouse)** to the bottom **(Basement)**, hitting everything **(All Floors and Rooms)** in between – **No Restrictions**. Conduct your Preflight Evaluation the same way.

Basement |⸺

The OODA Loop Revisited

Imagine you had 10 minutes to design your next iteration, using The OODA Loop as the model. That's 2 ½ minutes for each part of The Loop. What would that look like, and how long would it take? Let's review, below.

OBSERVE For the relevant areas of Evaluation, what are the improvements? What are the lessons learned? What were the false assumptions, surprises, and miscalculations? What are the Top 5 most impactful things that you are currently doing?

ORIENT For the areas of improvement, what are your options to improve them? For the lessons learned, what are your options to apply them? For the false assumptions, surprises, and miscalculations, what are your options to neutralize them? What should you continue doing, what should you stop doing, and what are the Objectives?

DECIDE For each Objective, what options do you choose? What is the impact of each option on, not just its area of influence, but the performance of the entire construct? To Finalize, what are your decided on choices?

ACT Engage. Get Started. Get to Work. Execute.

Begin the Next Cycle

You've heard this part before, but I'll repeat it. You've done the work. You've put in the time. You've created The Plan. Now, get to work. Take Action. Be focused and resilient. Even if your plan is not a perfect one, keep moving forward. You can fix any minor perfections on the next iteration. No Thing will ever be the perfect thing. No Time will ever be the perfect time. But, even though, what you have created is not a perfect thing, it is a Good Thing. And, even though it is not the perfect time, it is the Right Time. **Good Luck, on your next steps! Thanks, for listening.**

THE BEST TIME TO HAVE GOTTEN STARTED WITH ANYTHING WAS Now!

— CHARLES HODGE

FISICALITY

SECTION 7

BAGGAGE CLAIM

Lost Luggage and Unclaimed Freight

It's Game Time

Get started on the things you want to see happen now, rather than waiting for the perfect time. Waiting is like saying you'll start working out and eating right, sometime after you've gotten in shape. Waiting to invest until you have more money is like saying you'll start practicing for football season, just as soon as the ref is doing the coin toss for the first game. You haven't practiced, you're out of shape, you don't know the plays, you don't know how you're going to react under duress, and you don't even fully know the rules of the game, but you're going to wait until game day to jump right in.

Discipline Your Thoughts or Be Disciplined by Them

Thoughts and words are very powerful. Don't allow negative thoughts to run rampant, or negative realities will manifest. You can have negative thoughts, as their existence is often out of your control, but their subsequent influence is not out of your control. Think it, and then speak out loud the reality you want to see realized.

Money Doesn't Burn Holes in Steel Pockets

The other end of the spectrum from the Uninformed Savers, who save with no plan or goal in mind, are the Heedless Spenders, who spend in the same fashion. They often are not wasteful on purpose. Some people can't have money. They've got to do something with it. If they haven't preallocated it to something or don't have a plan, they spend it, blow it, or give it away. They psychologically can't handle knowing they have money available. They look for somewhere to place it with no good reason to do so. These people are the ones who actually have what it takes to become very skilled with Money Management. It bothers them to have money sitting idle. They want to put it to work. They don't necessarily want to spend it. It may SEEM that way, due to spending being a common chosen option, if they lack the experience and knowledge to wisely manage it. But, if you give these folks just an inkling of a plan and sensible justification on why that plan makes sense, they typically excel at personal finance.

Hodgerian Waterworks and Money Quirks

The linguistic relationship between water and money is unmistakable, even if I disregard Jordan Maxwell and his lambasting of society's Maritime/Admiralty Law ignorance (XVONE, 2022). **Money** is like **water** that **flows** from one place to another on a **river**, towards the **sea**. On a **flowing** river, when you have something you want to keep **safe** for later, you put it on the river's **bank**. If there were someone on the **riverbank** who could assist with the transfer of **assets** from the river to the bank and also secure those assets for us, in **the bank's safe** place, until we needed them again, I guess we could call that person a **banker**. When your assets are in the bank, you can retrieve them, as needed, **liquidate** them, and put them back in **circulation**, to create **cash flow**. Sometimes, large **waves** of cash flow can impact things **downstream**, and even cause an often lauded, beneficial, **trickle-down** effect, but in reality, this beneficial, trickle-down effect rarely happens.

Rivers often flow into larger bodies of water, eventually making their way to the sea. This means that the bank controls the flow of **curren(t)cy**, using the **current** to the **sea**. **Currency** is meant to flow. With proper management, a modest **trickle** of money could turn into a financial **gusher**. And if you have a lot of money that **pours** in, your bank account will **overflow**, and you will be **swimming** in it. However, safe and secure swimming is often best enjoyed in a **pool**, which unlike the sea, has gentle **ebbs and flows**. It's important to not become complacent with the false security of having a large **pool of money** though, because **tides** turn, which could reverse **fortune**. So, if you're not careful, those unchecked **drops** of money will **slip through your fingers**, just like water. If you make further mistakes and start **draining** your resources, all of your funds could **dry up**. This type of money **leak** can also happen in a stock market **bubble** that eventually pops, resulting in rapidly **sinking** prices which can sometimes **tank** the entire market.

Or, if you accumulate a lot of liabilities, you'll find yourself **underwater** and **drowning in debt**. This may result in your having to **shell** out a lot of **clams**, or being unable to **tap** into or use your money, if it has been **frozen** in order to satisfy your obligations. You might even need to go so far as to close the **flood gates**, to control the **storm surge** and create a **reservoir**. When that happens, it's important to keep your **head above water** and remain **buoyant**, until you can **shore** up your position. Hopefully, you've prepared for this type of situation and have some money on **ice**, set aside in reserve. This money is not quite frozen and not quite liquid, because it's sitting in your **slush fund**. With your slush fund, even if you don't have a huge **bucket** of money, you can still use it in a **DRIP** account to **rehydrate** a position. And, if you can **weather** the **storm**, eventually your **ship will come in**, and you'll get a **boatload** of **clams**. But, will your account eventually "Get Low"? Nah, your account will instead explode, from the Windows (Computer) to the Wall (Street) — so then you can **make it rain**, yet again. **Aww, skeet, skeet, skeet, skeet . . .**

Lost Luggage and Unclaimed Freight (Cont.)

It's Getting' Hottt in Herre

Stop putting wood in the flames, if you want the fire to go out.

The Haves and the Have-Mores

I can't speak for the rest of the world, but we in the U.S.A. have earned, been given, and taken the best and most of everything. We are very fortunate to have been born Americans. Collectively, we enjoy unprecedented wealth, autonomy, opportunity, resources, access to technology, access to knowledge, privilege, comfort, freedom, and status. And, we are doing everything in our power to destroy it. We abuse and pervert our entitlements, losing perspective on the price it took to receive our boon and the cost it takes to keep it. To restate Nightingale's allegory, we sit freezing, beside a woodpile, in front of a cold stove, chastising it with our admonition to heat up, telling it that if it first provides us with some heat, then we will light a flame and give it some wood. The Goose of Chance has given us an exorbitant amount of golden nuggets, but our entitlement, foolishness, and insolence has set us well on our way to sacrificing that goose, because it's blocking our view of those pretty eggs.

I.Q. Tesses

Intelligence and judgment are not the same thing. Intelligence Affluence frequently fuels Conceit, which results in Judgment Erosion. It's always stanktastic when someone knows a lot of stuff about a lot of stuff but is too stupid to make good decisions with it.

Golden's Rule

Get something on your naked mind – NAKED!!!

It Might Be Christmas-Style Time

If somebody from New Mexico approaches you and says, "Red or Green", it is a question and not a statement. And, the answer is "Green". It's always "Green". If you don't say, "Green", you might have to get down from the car and defend yourself.

Devil Hodge

For decades now, people have questioned me and accussed me of all sorts of things, because of my consistent use of various devil motifs and imagery. There is nothing esoterically sinister about it. My father's nickname is "Devil Hodge". The devil motif, imagery, and "The Hodge Angry Eye" (a stylized logo version of my actual eye), found in all of my productions is an admiration and respect callout to him.

Definition: accussed – using cussing, to accuse and fuss about something

FISICALITY

SECTION 8

Fisicality Distillation – Fiscal

FISICALITY ROADMAP

I. Figure out how much money you have right now.

II. Figure out from where, when, and how much money you THINK you're going to be getting in the future.

III. Set aside ICS (In Case Stuff) money.

IV. Figure out your Razor Result.
1. Figure out who you owe, how much, and the terms (balance, fees, penalties).
2. Figure out what you spend your money on each month.
3. Figure out how much money you're wasting (fees, penalties, buying dumb stuff, buying rubbish you don't use, etc.).
4. Determine your absolute minimum amount to live on – THIS IS YOUR RAZOR RESULT.
5. Subtract your Razor Result from the amount of money you have coming in for the month – THIS IS YOUR AFTER SHAVE RESULT.

V. Plan how you want to distribute the After Shave money.
1. Pay off debts by ranking from smallest to largest and from highest interest to lowest interest.
2. Establish pay percentages for debt payoff and wealth accumulation categories.
3. Prioritize payoff for all high interest and revolving debt.
4. Fully fund ICS account.
5. Start funding Emergency Account.
6. Establish a working savings cushion (equal to one month's worth of bills owed).
7. Start funding HSA.
8. Establish 401K match contribution.
9. Establish initial IRA fund.
10. Establish initial investment portfolio and protocols.
11. Fully fund HSA.
12. Fully fund 401K.
13. Fully fund IRA.
14. Expand investment portfolio.

FOUNDATIONAL PRINCIPLES

I. Analogue.
1. Learn the basics of using a physical, accounting ledger. Using a physical book, even for a short while, can give you skills and comfort with financial tracking that easily transfers to the digital arena.
2. If cash usage is high, create an envelope system where distinct, labeled envelopes are filled with corresponding bill payment amounts. Once a bill is paid, refill each envelope, as needed. Spend envelope money, only according to its label.

II. Digital.
1. Learn the basics of how the financial system operates with Ray Dalio's "How the Economic Machine Works" at:
    https://www.youtube.com/watch?v=PHe0bXAIuk0
2. Learn the details of the debt crisis with Jonathan Jarvis' "The Crisis of Credit Visualized" at:
    https://www.youtube.com/watch?v=bx_LWm6_6tA
3. Learn two popular methods for paying off debt with Next Level Life's "Debt Snowball vs Debt Avalanche" at:
    https://www.youtube.com/watch?v=jtgnRJKSJlw
4. Learn about the power of compound interest with Next Level Life's "The Power of Compound Interest" at:
    https://www.youtube.com/watch?v=wtAB-Zg_79I

CREATE THE FISCAL PROFILE

In order to determine your fiscal health, gather the foundational information for the following: Credit Reports, ChexSystems Report, Social Security Report, Net Worth Report, and your Razor Report. Information about each criterion is detailed below.

I. Credit Report.
According to the Federal Trade Commission at https://www.ftc.gov/, you're entitled to one free copy of your credit report every 12 months from each of the three nationwide credit reporting companies, Equifax, TransUnion, and Experian. You will need to provide your name, address, social security number, and date of birth to verify your identity. Call 1-877-322-8228, or order online from the only authorized website for free credit reports here: https://www.annualcreditreport.com/.

II. ChexSystems Report.
Under the Fair and Accurate Credit Transaction Act (FACTA) amendments to the Federal Fair Credit Reporting Act (FCRA), you are entitled to request a free copy of your ChexSystems consumer report, once every 12 months. Call

1-800-428-9623, or order your ChexSystems Consumer Disclosure and Consumer Score reports online, here: https://www.chexsystems.com/.

III. LexisNexis Report.
Under the Fair and Accurate Credit Transaction Act (FACTA) amendments to the Federal Fair Credit Reporting Act (FCRA), you are entitled to request a free copy of all of your LexisNexis consumer reports, once every 12 months. Call 1-888-497-0011, or order online, for your free LexisNexis Consumer Disclosure Report and Description of Procedure Letter, here: https://consumer.risk.lexisnexis.com/request.

IV. Social Security Report.
Generate a report on your lifetime recorded earnings with the Social Security Administration that shows the Work Year, Taxed Social Security Earnings, and Taxed Medicare Earnings here: https://secure.ssa.gov/.

V. Net Worth Report.
Generate a report on your current Net Worth by subtracting all of your Liabilities from all of your Assets. To assist, you can use the Omni Net Worth Calculator here: https://www.omnicalculator.com/.

VI. Paycheck Capture.
Create an export of all data from your paycheck every other month.

VII. Razor Results.
Generate a report on your current absolute minimum money required to live with zero luxuries, extras, non-essentials, comforts, or peripherals. Subtract all of your Monthly Debits from all of your Monthly Credits. To assist, you can use the Omni Budget Calculator here: https://www.omnicalculator.com/.

DATA CONSOLIDATION AND MANAGEMENT
Consolidate all your data requested by The Ignition Page. Create a copy, use, and edit as necessary, the Fisicality Financial Management spreadsheet here: Fisicality Financial Management Spreadsheet.

I. Types Of Sample Budgets.
1. Percentage
2. Value
3. Hard Copy
4. Automatic
5. Comprehensive
6. Reverse
7. VIDEO: 6 Types of Budgets Explained

II.   Potential Budget Ledgers.

1. Fisicality Spreadsheet: HH Fisicality
2. Personal Capital: https://www.personalcapital.com/
3. Mint: https://www.mint.com/
4. YNAB: https://www.youneedabudget.com/

Fisicality Distillation – Anabolic

ANABOLIC ROADMAP

I. Simplify Everything.
1. There are no shortcuts.
2. Take the Long Route on the Hard Road.
3. Put in the Work.

II. Eat Big.
1. Eat enough to gain a minimum of a pound a week, to start.
2. Eat simple foods that look like what they are.
3. Eat a minimum of 1 gram of protein per pound of body weight.
4. Drink water until your urine looks like diluted lemonade.
5. Spend the money you were going to buy supplements with on eggs, beef, and full fat whole milk.
6. Avoid vegetable oils, simple carbohydrates, and sugar.
7. Eat crayon box vegetables (lots of colors).
8. Eat 3 times a day, and don't snack in between.

III. Sleep Big.
1. Sleep until you feel rested.
2. Replace an activity with sleep, if you feel unrested.
3. Take frequent naps.
4. Skip partying, late nights, and empty, high energy activities.

IV. Lift Big.
1. Workout 3 days a week.
2. Warm up.
3. Be extra cautious loading and unloading weight.
4. Be extra cautious on the first rep and last rep of any set.
5. Be extra cautious unracking and reracking the weight.
6. Use the first set to dial in rep cadence, angles, depth, and balance.
7. Do not use a full range of motion on the first rep of any set.
8. Focus on big, basic compound movements.
9. Do 3-5 Work Sets, the last 1-2 to failure, for each exercise.
10. Try to add weight, even small amounts, as often as possible.
11. Perform 12 reps, for each exercise. If given a choice to add weight or add reps to increase intensity, add weight.
12. Use Drop Sets and Rest-Pause, when your Cock Diesel Meter is high.
13. Come back from injuries slowly. Workout around injuries, using lighter weights with strict form. Your brain will tell you what you can't do. Your body will let you know what you might be able to do. Your mind can override both of them, to do what you didn't think you could do.

V. Think Big.

1. Get comfortable with being uncomfortable.
2. Don't whine or complain – Nobody Cares.
3. Be relaxed but serious when lifting.
4. Think about your workout, before heading to the gym.
5. Steel your resolve to endure discomfort and perform in excellent fashion, under duress.
6. Research nutrition, exercise techniques, and health topics.
7. Read the Robert E. Howard "Conan the Barbarian" novels.
8. Read Napoleon Hill's "The Strangest Secret".
9. Heavy iron is your friend; heavy iron is your foe. Use the teachings in the books above to deal with it.

Understand that you won't truly know what your True Limit is, with ANYTHING in life, until something Breaks. If nothing has Broken, you haven't reached your Limit.

SAMPLE WORKOUT - Peer Muscle Groupings that work the same body parts are Workouts 1 & 3 and Workouts 2 & 4. A full cycle to complete all exercises will require 4 workout days. This means a Muscle Grouping will be hit twice one week and once the next, alternating frequency with the other Muscle Grouping. Using the routine below, do not workout on consecutive days, and do not workout more than 3 days per week.

WEEK 1:   **MON** - Workout 1   **WED** - Workout 2   **FRI** - Workout 3
WEEK 2:   **MON** - Workout 4   **WED** - Workout 1   **FRI** - Workout 2

Workout 1

1. Squat
2. Bench Press
3. Chest Supported Row
4. Military Press
5. Dumbbell Rear Delt

Workout 2

1. Deadlift
2. Romanian Deadlift
3. Barbell Curl
4. Dips
5. Standing Calf Raise

Workout 3

1. Leg Press
2. Incline Press
3. Pull-Up/Chin-Up
4. Seated Shoulder Press
5. Dumbbell Lateral Delt

Workout 4

1. Trap Bar Deadlift
2. Hamstring Curl
3. Dumbbell Curl
4. Lying Tricep Extension
5. Seated Calf Raise

FISICALITY

SECTION 9

INFORMATION DESK

TERMINOLOGY - FISCAL

Alpha - Term used to describe the return on an investment that's above the return of the overall market, a section of the market, an index, or a defined benchmark. It's the market volatility adjusted return above the predicted benchmark return.

Bagholder - Someone who held on to a losing investment, as its price plunged. The investment is one whose prospects are bleak or whose recovery to break even will take a long time.

Bear - A pessimistic investor who thinks stocks or major indexes will decrease by ~20% or more. Bearish sentiment is specific. For example, a bear can believe that the market is going to crash by 20%, while also believing that a single stock or sector within the market is going to run up by 30%.

Black Swan - An extremely rare, unpredictable event that may happen only once in a generation or once in a lifetime that usually has severe impacts and extreme consequences, on financial markets. Examples of this type of event include the COVID-19 pandemic and the 2008 Global Financial Crisis.

Blue Chip - A large market cap company with a good reputation, excellent management, and sound financials. It is usually a top 3 company for its industry and has proven its resilience to economic downturns, stock volatility, and market stress. Examples of this type of company include Coca-Cola, McDonald's, Microsoft, and Lockheed Martin.

Book Value - The book value for an item is determined when all of its liabilities are subtracted from all of its tangible assets. It is conceptually similar to an individual's net worth.

Bubble - A condition where the price of an asset, stock, asset class, market, or sector is significantly more than its actual value. Bubbles are often driven by euphoria and FOMO.

Bull - An optimistic investor who thinks stocks or major indexes will increase by ~20% or more. Bullish sentiment is specific. For example, a bull can believe that the market is going to rise by 40%, while also believing that a single stock or sector within the market is going to crash by 25%.

Cash Flow Statement - A summary of the cash inflows and outflows of a company, for a given fiscal period.

Common Stock - Publicly listed, exchange traded shares of company stock that any common man can buy. Shareholders are typically given voting rights.

Dead Cat Bounce - Refers to a stock that is crashing and on its way to irrelevancy that has a sudden sharp rise, before it quickly falls again.

Dip - A momentary drop in an asset's price. This element is often sought out by investors who want to pay a lower price for a higher quality stock, by "buying the dip".

EBITDA - Term stands for earnings before interest, taxes, depreciation, and amortization. It is a measure of a company's profitability that excludes these expenses and can indicate if a company generates enough cash flow to cover expenses and debt payments.

Exchange - Marketplace where financial securities are traded. This may include commodities, exchange traded funds, derivatives, and other financial instruments.

FOMO - Term stands for Fear of Missing Out and describes the phenomenon of investors abandoning analysis and data driven decision making, in favor of emotion driven choices, to buy a popular or quickly rising security or sell one that's quickly falling.

Hedge - A type of stock portfolio diversification that seeks to neutralize risk of loss by acquiring shares new stocks that tend to trend in the opposite direction of currently owned investments.

HODL - Term stands for Hold On for Dear Life and describes the phenomenon where investors disregard all data about an owned security and refuse to sell it. At its most pure a HODL Investor will ride a security all the way down to $0.

Index Fund - An ETF or mutual fund that seeks to mirror the composition and performance of an existing benchmark or index.

Investment - Acquisition of an asset with the notion that it will increase in value, provide a realized benefit, or generate income over time.

OTC - Term stands for Over-the-Counter that describes the listing and trading of stocks directly between brokers and investors. These stocks are not listed on the two major stock exchanges in the U.S., the NYSE and the NASDAQ.

Penny Stock - Publicly listed, Over-the-Counter traded shares of company stock that any common man can buy that trades for less than $5.00 per share.

Play - Refers to the simple act of investing in a stock. A good play delivers the expected outcome, while a bad play does not.

Preferred Stock - Describes stock shares that, unlike shares of common stock, has a high claim on distributions and assets, but they normally don't have voting rights. If there is contention with distributions, the preferred stock will receive its full payout before the common stock receives any payout.

Pump and Dump - A term describing the illegal practice of a shareholder manipulating the market and artificially inflating the price of a cheaply bought stock and then selling the shares, at a greatly inflated price.

TERMINOLOGY - FISCAL (CONT.)

Seed Money - The initial funding used to form, create, or begin operations for a company, endeavor, or initiative. It usually conveys some kind of equity stake or other consideration to funding entity.

Short Squeeze - A rapid rise in price for a stock where investors predict that the stock will fall in price. Investors who invest predicting a fall in price lose money, if the stock price increases. These "short" investors typically exit their trades, in the price drop's "squeeze".

SWAN - Coined by Brad Thomas, the term stands for Sleep Well At Night. It embodies the notion that owned stock is for a company that is stable, increasing in value, income generating, large cap, and has a wide moat.

Value Investing - Disciplined investing strategy that seeks to buy quality stocks that are trading well below their intrinsic or book value.

Whale - An investor, investment group, bank, or trust whose trades are so large, they can influence market reactions, on their own.

TERMINOLOGY - ANABOLIC

ATG - A barbell squat performed where the lifter descends, so that the thighs go pass parallel and the hamstrings touch the calves. Reword "Fanny-to-Fescue" to get the full meaning.

Buffed - A refined, muscular body that has good balance, size, definition, and proportion that is aesthetically pleasing.

Burn - Working a muscle, until it's demand for oxygen outpaces the lungs ability to supply the oxygen needed for energy production. This causes lactic acid to be built up, creating a distinct burning sensation, in the worked muscle.

Cheating - Using loose form, advantageous angles, assistance paraphernalia, surrounding muscle groups, or momentum to complete reps of an exercise.

Cock Diesel - Describes a lifter who is exceptionally strong and usually much stronger than their size would indicate. The lifter may or may not be very large or muscular, but they will always exhibit a very high, pound-for-pound strength level.

Cutting - Purposefully losing body fat, while maintaining muscle mass, to increase muscle definition, striations, and vascularity.

Deads - Another term for deadlifts.

Drop Set - An intensity technique for an exercise set where the lifter completes a set to failure, immediately reduces or "drops" the weight, completes those reps to failure, and repeats, until they've reached their target intensity. A typical drop set can include as few as 1 and as many as 4-5 drops.

Dry Out - Lose excess body fluid through a combination of steady-state cardio, nutrient and mineral intake, and diuretics. The goal, when drying out, is to create a hard, chiseled look, with the physique.

Failure - Exercising a muscle with repeated reps in a set, until no additional reps can be performed with out compromising form, cheating, or getting external assistance.

Fast Twitch - Refers to the muscle fibers that are used in burst scenarios, like throwing a ball, sprinting, powerlifting, or explosive jumping.

Flex - The angle decrease of joint-connected bones that causes a shortening of the attached muscles.

Forced Rep - Repetitions perfomred with good form, after a lifter has reached failure, with the assistance of a person or machine spotter.

Free Weight - Weights that have no external attachment, stability, or leverage points, do not inherently restrict movement, and offer no balancing assistance, for a particular exercise.

Guns - Large, well defined, muscular arms.

Lats - Short for latissimus dorsi, the large, flaring, outer muscles of the back that can be seen from every angle of the human body.

Lock Out - The last few inches of the positive phase of a rep where the joint is fully extended or fully contracted. Some exercises start in the contracted position, such as the bench press or deadlift, while some start in the extended position, such as the barbell curl or barbell row.

Machine - Weights that have external attachment, stability, or leverage points, that follow predetermined paths, and assist with balance.

Mirin - Appreciating and acknowledging another lifter's accomplishments, in regards to strength, muscularity, or intensity.

Money Set - This is the last, most intense set of an exercise, during a workout. All the other sets and reps of an exercise were precursors used to prepare for this one, final set. Advanced lifters typically use intensity techniques, such as drop sets, rest pause, and assisted negatives, for the Money Set.

Muscularity - Describes the level of leanness and definition, most typically for a trained, developed body.

Negative - Describes the portion of the lift where the lifter is essentially "braking" or slowing the weight, as it return to the starting position.

Power - The ability to directly cause movement with something that is stationary, or cause a change in direction or speed with something that is moving. The calculation for it is: Power = Force x Velocity. A locomotive or hurricane are said to be powerful, but not strong, based on the influence they exert on environmental elements.

Pumped - The sensation and look of blood engorged muscles that have temporarily increased in size, due to high repetitions, full range of motion work, done with moderate weight.

Rep - Short for repetition, this term describes one lifter-defined, full range of motion, completed movement, from start to finish, for an exercise.

Ripped - Exhibiting extremely low bodyfat, high definition, abundant striations, high vascularity, and low fluid retention.

Slow Twitch - Refers to the muscle fibers that are used in plodding scenarios, like swimming, hiking, cycling, or distance running.

Spot, or Spotter - An assist given to a lifter to help them complete repetitions with good form, as they approach and reach failure, or the act of providing on-demand assistance, if needed, for safety,

TERMINOLOGY - ANABOLIC (CONT.)

Straps - Strips of durable, reinforced, cloth or leather that are wrapped around lifting equipment to assist with securing hand gripping.

Strength - The ability to directly statically hold something that is stationary or resist direction change or speed from something that is moving. The calculation for it is: Force = Mass x Acceleration. A bridge or a wall do not move but are said to be strong, not powerful, due to the amount of stress they can withstand, without distorting.

Striations - The condition of having the impressions and ridges of individual muscle fibers and small clusters of muscle fibers visible through the skin.

Superset - Performing two different exercises, back-to-back, with no rest between them is considered one superset.

Swole - A large, somewhat defined lifter who has an abundance of mass, tight skin, and full-looking muscle. They are not depleted and may have some fluid retention. Unlike the pump, the swole lifter maintains this look for weeks to months, at a time.

Wraps - Strips of durable, reinforced, elastic cloth that are wrapped around joints, muscles, or limbs to provide additional support, particularly on maximum lifting attempts or injured areas.

Yoked - A lifter with decent, overall muscularity and size, but who specifically has an exceptional amount of development in their shoulders, traps, and back (the yoke area). Here, think of oxen with their large muscular necks and backs that are often "yoked", to perform work.

SOURCES

Abelsson, Andreas. (2023, March 28). "Protein Requirements by Age: A Complete Guide". Strength Log. Retrieved July 12, 2024 from, https://www.strengthlog.com/protein-requirements-by-age/

Alves, R., Prestes, J., Enes, A., de Moraes, W., Trindade, T., de Salles, B., Aragon, A., Souza-Junior, T. (2020). "Training Programs Designed for Muscle Hypertrophy in Bodybuilders: A Narrative Review". Retrieved July 08, 2024 from, https://www.mdpi.com/2075-4663/8/11/149

Barnum, P.T. (2023). "The Art of Money Getting." Internet Archive. Retrieved June 26, 2024 from, https://archive.org/details/p-t-barnum_the-art-of-money-getting_202302/mode/2up (Original work published 1888)

Bauer, P., Majisik, A., Mitter, B., Csapo, R., Tschan, H., Hume, P., Martínez-Rodríguez, A., Makivic, B. (2023, March). "Body Composition of Competitive Bodybuilders: A Systematic Review of Published Data and Recommendations for Future Work". Journal of Strength and Conditioning Research. Retrieved July 16, 2024 from, https://journals.lww.com/nsca-jscr/abstract/2023/03000/body_composition_of_competitive_bodybuilders__a.23.aspx

Black, Michelle. (2024, July 29). "What Is The Average Credit Card Interest Rate This Week? July 30, 2024". Forbes Advisor. Retrieved July 30, 2024 from, https://www.forbes.com/advisor/credit-cards/average-credit-card-interest-rate/

Boyd, John. (1995, June 28). "The Essence of Winning and Losing (Chuck Spinney, Chet Richards & Ginger Richards, Ed.)". Colonel John Boyd. Retrieved June 25, 2024 from, https://www.coljohnboyd.com/static/documents/1995-06-28__Boyd_John_R__The_Essence_of_Winning_and_Losing__PPT-PDF.pdf

Branchereau, Gaël. (2017, September 30). "Freud and the Nobel Trauma". The Jakarta Post. Retrieved August 13, 2024 from, https://www.thejakartapost.com/life/2017/09/30/freud-and-the-nobel-trauma.html

Bureau of Labor Statistics. (2024, April 4). "Occupational Employment and Wage Statistics". U.S. Bureau of Labor Statistics. Retrieved August 13, 2024 from, https://www.bls.gov/oes/current/oes_nat.htm

Canadian Conservation Institute. (2020, January 7). "Longevity of Recordable CDs, DVDs and Blu-rays – Canadian Conservation Institute (CCI) Notes 19/1". Canadian Conservation Institute. Retrieved July 20 2024 from, https://www.canada.ca/en/conservation-institute/services/conservation-preservation-publications/canadian-conservation-institute-notes/longevity-recordable-cds-dvds.html

CFPB. (2019, August). "The Consumer Credit Card Market". Bureau of Consumer Financial Protection. Retrieved June 27, 2024 from, https://files.consumerfinance.gov/f/documents/cfpb_consumer-credit-card-market-report_2019.pdf

Chittenden, Lucius. (1891). "Recollections of President Lincoln and His Administration". Harper & Brothers.

Companies Marketcap. (2024). "Top publicly traded American companies by number of employees". Companies Market Cap. Retrieved August 24, 2024 from, https://companiesmarketcap.com/usa/largest-american-companies-by-number-of-employees/

Consumer Financial Protection Bureau. (2023, October). "The Consumer Credit Card Market". Retrieved June 26, 2024 from, https://files.consumerfinance.gov/f/documents/cfpb_consumer-credit-card-market-report_2023.pdf

Desjardins, Jeff. (2016, August 4). "Chart: 14% of Americans Have Negative Wealth. " Visual Capitalist. Retrieved June 25, 2024 from, https://www.visualcapitalist.com/14-percent-americans-negative-wealth/

Dhariwal, Abhishek. (2022, October 24). "'He's Stronger and Stuff Like That…': 2X DPOY Dennis Rodman Revealed the Toughest Opponents He Faced in His NBA Career in 2021". EssentiallySports. Retrieved July 18, 2024 from, https://www.essentiallysports.com/nba-basketball-news-hes-stronger-and-stuff-like-that-2x-dpoy-dennis-rodman-revealed-the-toughest-opponents-he-faced-in-his-nba-career-in-2021/

Freud, Sigmund. (1922). "Beyond the Pleasure Principle (C. J. M. Hubback, Trans.)". The International Psycho-Analytical Press. (Original work published 1922)

Gatollari, Mustafa. (2018). "The Story Behind 'Home Alone's Fake Movie Within a Movie, 'Angels With Filthy Souls'". Distractify. Retrieved July 09, 2024 from, https://www.distractify.com/entertainment/2018/12/26/Ce93hrA/home-alone-angels-with-filthy-souls

Grant, James. (1983). "Bernard M. Baruch. "The Adventures of a Wall Street Legend". Simon and Schuster.

Gries, K., Raue, U., Perkins, R., Lavin, K., Overstreet, B., D'Acquisito, L., Graham, B., Finch, W., Kaminsky, L., Trappe, T., Trappe, S. (2018, August, 22). "Cardiovascular and skeletal muscle health with lifelong exercise". Human Performance Laboratory, Ball State University, Muncie, Indiana. Retrieved July 15, 2024 from, https://journals.physiology.org/doi/epdf/10.1152/japplphysiol.00174.2018

Hinkle, Mark. (2021). "Social Security Board of Trustees: Combined Trust Funds

Projected Depletion One Year Sooner Than Last Year". Social Security Administration. Retrieved June 26, 2024 from, https://www.ssa.gov/news/press/releases/2021/#8-2021-2

Hodge, Charles. (2019, August 12). "Systems Engineering: 2020 Operational Blueprint". Integrated Vertical Technology, LLC. https://www.amazon.com/

Horymski, Chris. (2024, February 14). "Experian Study: Average U.S. Consumer Debt and Statistics". Experian. Retrieved June 26, 2024 from, https://www.experian.com/blogs/ask-experian/research/consumer-debt-study/

HUD Exchange. (n.d.). "Homeless Definition". US Department of Housing and Urban Development. Retrieved June 27, 2024 from, https://files.hudexchange.info/resources/documents/HomelessDefinition_RecordkeepingRequirementsandCriteria.pdf

IRS Publication 550. (2023, March 8). "Investment Income and Expenses (Including Capital Gains and Losses)". Internal Revenue Service. Retrieved June 27, 2024 from, https://www.irs.gov/pub/irs-pdf/p550.pdf

Kasdan, Lawrence (Director). (1994). "Wyatt Earp" [Film]. Kasdan Pictures and Tig Productions.Kerr-Dineen, Luke. (2023, August 23). "Gary Player said this golf swing 'improvement' gained him 30 yards". GolfDigest. Retrieved July 09, 2024 from, https://www.golfdigest.com/story/gary-player-golf-swing-distance-improvement-30-yards

M-Disk. (2019). "M-Disk Technology". M-Disk. Retrieved July 29, 2024 from, https://www.mdisc.com/technology.html

Machiavelli, Niccolò. (1981). "The Prince" (Daniel Donno, Trans.). Bantam Books. (Original work published 1513)

McDonald, M., Loggins, K. (1978). "What a Fool Believes" [Song recorded by The Doobie Brothers]. On "Minute by Minute" [Album]. Warner Bros.

McMahon,Tim. (2024, July 11). "What is the Current Inflation Rate?". InflationData. Retrieved July 26, 2024 from, https://inflationdata.com/Inflation/Inflation_Rate/CurrentInflation.asp?reloaded=true.

McRaney, David. (2011). "You Are Not So Smart". Avery an Imprint of Penguin Random House LLC.

Meyer, Chris. (n.d.). "11 Philosophical Razors to Simplify Your Life". The Mind Collection. Retrieved June 26, 2024 from, https://themindcollection.com/philosophical-razors/

Mountainside. (n.d.). "Happy Hormones and the Science of Addiction". Mountainside Treatment Center. Retrieved June 25,2024 from https://

mountainside.com/blog/mental-health/happy-hormones-and-the-science-of-addiction/

myFICO. (n.d.). "What's in my FICO® Scores?" Fair Isaac Corporation. Retrieved June 26, 2024 from, https://www.myfico.com/credit-education/whats-in-your-credit-score

Nabi, Shehryar. (2022, May 25). "Thirteen million US households have negative net worth. Will they ever move from debt to wealth?". The Aspen Institute. Retrieved August 13, 2024 from, https://www.aspeninstitute.org/blog-posts/thirteen-million-us-households-have-negative-net-worth-will-they-ever-move-from-debt-to-wealth/

Nightingale, Earl. (2006). "The Strangest Secret" [Audio recording] (W., Deena, Transcriber.). BN Publishing. (Original work recorded 1956)

NIST. (2023, October 16). "NIST Special Publication 800-63B Digital Identity Guidelines: Authentication and Lifecycle Management". U.S. Department of Commerce. Retrieved June 26, 2024 from, https://pages.nist.gov/800-63-3/sp800-63b.html

NLIHC. (2024). "Out of Reach: The High Cost of Housing". National Low Income Housing Coalition. Retrieved July 26, 2024 from, https://nlihc.org/sites/default/files/2024_OOR.pdf

Nuckols, Greg. (n.d.). "Bench Press Bar Path: How to Fix Your Bar Path for a Bigger Bench". Stronger by Science. Retrieved July 09, 2024 from, https://www.strongerbyscience.com/bench-press-bar-path/

Paystub. (2023, June 30). "The Complete Guide to Pay Stub Requirements by State". Form Source, LLC. Retrieved June 26, 2024 from, https://paystub.org/posts/pay-stub-requirements-by-state

Petrosyan, Ani. (2024, March 6). "Number of victims of data violation incidents in the United States from 2022 to 2023, by industry (in millions)". Statista. Retrieved June 26, 2024 from, https://www.statista.com/statistics/1454890/us-number-of-data-compromise-victims-by-industry/

Petrosyan, Ani. (2024, April 11). "American adults on probability of them encountering financial cybercrime in the future as of September 2023". Statista. Retrieved June 26, 2024 from, https://www.statista.com/statistics/1460464/financial-cybercrime-fraud-victim-likelihood/

Press, Gil. (2024, February 4). "Internet Traffic from Mobile Devices Stats (2024)". What'stheBigData. Retrieved June 26, 2024 from, https://whatsthebigdata.com/mobile-internet-traffic/

Richter, Daniel. (2023, November 2). "Top 10 Strength Training Statistics From

Half a Million Users of Our Workout Log". Strength Log. Retrieved July 12. 2024 from, https://www.strengthlog.com/strength-training-statistics/

Rodman, D., Keown, Tim. (1996). "Bad as I Want to Be". Delacorte Press/Bantam Doubleday Dell Publishing Group, Inc.

Scherer, Zachary. (2023, November). "Social Security: 20221 - Survey of Income and Program Participation Snapshots). U.S. Census Bureau. Retrieved July 29, 2024 from https://www.census.gov/content/dam/Census/library/factsheets/2022/demo/p70fs-188.pdf

Scott, Elizabeth. (2022, June 23). "Hedonic Adaptation: Why You Are Not Happier". Verywell Mind. Retrieved June 25, 2024 from, https://www.verywellmind.com/hedonic-adaptation-4156926

Sharma, Nikhil. (2008, February 4). "The Origin of Data Information Knowledge Wisdom (DIKW) Hierarchy". ResearchGate. Retrieved August 12, 2024 from, https://www.researchgate.net/publication/292335202_The_Origin_of_Data_Information_Knowledge_Wisdom_DIKW_Hierarchy

Social Security Administration Board of Trustees. (2021). "2021 Annual Report of the Board of Trustees of the Federal Old-Age and Survivors Insurance and Federal Disability Insurance Trust Funds. Retrieved June 26, 2024 from, https://www.ssa.gov/OACT/TR/2021/tr2021.pdf

The Football Odyssey. (2020, July 14). "The History of Strength and Conditioning Coaches in Football". Retrieved July 10, 2024 from, https://www.thefootballodyssey.com/gridiron-outliers/the-history-of-strength-and-conditioning-coaches

TipRanks. (2024). "Dollar Cost Averaging Calculator". Retrieved July 15, 2024 from, https://www.tipranks.com/personal-finance/investing-and-retirement/dollar-cost-averaging?ticker=SPY&startYear=2014&period=month&startMonth=7&endMonth=7&endYear=2024&monthlyInvestment=200&initialInvestment=0&multipleRecurringInvestmentOnChange=0.01&multipleRecurringInvestment=1

Verizon. (2018, April 11). "2018 Data Breach Investigations Report 11th Edition". ResearchGate. Retrieved June 26, 2024 from, https://www.researchgate.net/publication/324455350_2018_Verizon_Data_Breach_Investigations_Report

Wikipedia. (2024, May 14). "DIKW Pyramid." Retrieved June 25, 2024 from, https://en.wikipedia.org/wiki/DIKW_pyramid

XVONE. (2022, June 22). "Jordan Maxwell - MARITIME ADMIRALTY LAW Full Lecture (Death 2022 RIP)" [Video]. YouTube. https://www.youtube.com/watch?v=HCedeAskim4

INDEX

IMAGE ATTRIBUTION

60, Envato Elements Pty Ltd, bartama_graphic, Idea 3D Icon
60, Envato Elements Pty Ltd, imoogigraphic, Multitasking Scene 3D Character
61, Charles Hodge - IVT Press, Charles Hodge, Battery Meter
61, Envato Elements Pty Ltd, PixelSquid360, Cartoon Fries
61, Envato Elements Pty Ltd, PixelSquid360, Hamburger
62, Envato Elements Pty Ltd, Libersla, Basketball Player Mascot
62, Envato Elements Pty Ltd, PixelSquid360, Check Mark Green
62, Envato Elements Pty Ltd, PixelSquid360, Cola Glass
62, Envato Elements Pty Ltd, PixelSquid360, X Shape
64, Envato Elements Pty Ltd, PixelSquid360, Body Build Gym Exercise Health
65, Envato Elements Pty Ltd, esysyarof, Fitness 3D Icon
65, Envato Elements Pty Ltd, PixelSquid360, Golf Tee And Ball On A Grass
67, Charles Hodge - IVT Press, Charles Hodge, OODA
68, Envato Elements Pty Ltd, PixelSquid360, Body Build Gym Exercise Health
69, Envato Elements Pty Ltd, esysyarof, Fitness 3D Icon
70, Envato Elements Pty Ltd, deviap366, Accounting 3D Icon
70, Envato Elements Pty Ltd, ekatastudio, Cloud Computing 3D Icons
70, Envato Elements Pty Ltd, ekatastudio, Cloud Computing 3D Icons
73, Envato Elements Pty Ltd, spacestudios, Banking 3D Icon
74, Envato Elements Pty Ltd, PixelSquid360, Body Build Gym Exercise Health
75, Envato Elements Pty Ltd, esysyarof, Fitness 3D Icon
76, Envato Elements Pty Ltd, esysyarof, Fitness 3D Icon
76, Envato Elements Pty Ltd, koctia, 120 Business Doodle Icons
77, Envato Elements Pty Ltd, Icons8, Fluent system filled - Shields
78, Envato Elements Pty Ltd, deviap366, Accounting 3D Icon
78, Envato Elements Pty Ltd, EklipStudio, Accounting 3D Icon Set
78, Envato Elements Pty Ltd, permadicreative, Accounting 3D Icon
79, Charles Hodge - IVT Press, Charles Hodge, Budget
80, Envato Elements Pty Ltd, PixelSquid360, Body Build Gym Exercise Health
81, Envato Elements Pty Ltd, esysyarof, Fitness 3D Icon
81, Envato Elements Pty Ltd, sparklethings, Data Management 3D Icon Pack
84, Envato Elements Pty Ltd, sparklethings, Data Management 3D Icon Pack
84, Envato Elements Pty Ltd, sparklethings, Data Management 3D Icon Pack
86, Envato Elements Pty Ltd, PixelSquid360, Body Build Gym Exercise Health
87, Envato Elements Pty Ltd, esysyarof, Fitness 3D Icon
87, Envato Elements Pty Ltd, orenjistudio, Boy Climbing Ladder While Holding Jigsaw Piece
87, Envato Elements Pty Ltd, PixelSquid360, Colorful Puzzle Head
88, Envato Elements Pty Ltd, PixelSquid360, Light Bulb Icon
88, Envato Elements Pty Ltd, sparklethings, Education 3D Icon Pack
88, Envato Elements Pty Ltd, StringLabs, Tools and Equipments 3D Illustration Set
88, Envato Elements Pty Ltd, Vektorastudio, Supermarket 3D Illustration
88, Envato Elements Pty Ltd, Vianor, Miscellany 3D Icons
90, Envato Elements Pty Ltd, PixelSquid360, Cartoon Hand
90, Envato Elements Pty Ltd, PixelSquid360, Body Build Gym Exercise Health
93, Envato Elements Pty Ltd, EklipStudio, Accounting 3D Icon Set
94, Envato Elements Pty Ltd, Vektorastudio, Money 3D Illustration
96, Envato Elements Pty Ltd, alexdndz, Banking Isometric Outline Illustration
97, Envato Elements Pty Ltd, PixelSquid360, Boxing Glove
98, Envato Elements Pty Ltd, PixelSquid360, Body Build Gym Exercise Health
99, Envato Elements Pty Ltd, Algrafika_Official, Gym and Fitness 3D Icon
99, Envato Elements Pty Ltd, deviap366, GYM and Fitness 3D Icon
99, Envato Elements Pty Ltd, esysyarof, Fitness 3D Icon
100, Envato Elements Pty Ltd, enesyk, USA Maps PowerPoint Templates
101, Envato Elements Pty Ltd, imoogigraphic, Server Maintenance 3D Character
101, Envato Elements Pty Ltd, RakataStudio, Online Data Security Interface 3D

101, Envato Elements Pty Ltd, uigodesign, Hardware 3D Icon
101, Envato Elements Pty Ltd, Vektorastudio, Money 3D Illustration
107, Envato Elements Pty Ltd, PixelSquid360, Egg Container
107, Envato Elements Pty Ltd, PixelSquid360, Egg In Cup
107, Envato Elements Pty Ltd, PixelSquid360, Egg Tray With Eggs
107, Envato Elements Pty Ltd, PixelSquid360, Eggs
107, Envato Elements Pty Ltd, PixelSquid360, Eggs Brown in Box
109, Envato Elements Pty Ltd, konkapp, 30 Trees Icons
110, Envato Elements Pty Ltd, PixelSquid360, Body Build Gym Exercise Health
111, Envato Elements Pty Ltd, esysyarof, Fitness 3D Icon
111, Envato Elements Pty Ltd, PixelSquid360, Sports Mannequin Male Silver
112, Envato Elements Pty Ltd, ekatastudio, Cloud Computing 3D Icons
113, Envato Elements Pty Ltd, ekatastudio, Cloud Computing 3D Icons
113, Envato Elements Pty Ltd, ekatastudio, Cloud Computing 3D Icons
113, Envato Elements Pty Ltd, EklipStudio, Accounting 3D Icon Set
113, Envato Elements Pty Ltd, RakataStudio, Smart Security 3D Illustration
113, Envato Elements Pty Ltd, spacestudios, Banking 3D Icon
114, Envato Elements Pty Ltd, PixelSquid360, Cartoon Hand
115, Envato Elements Pty Ltd, BasicLayout, Finance & Money 3D Icon Pack
115, Envato Elements Pty Ltd, Krafted, 3D Real Estate Icons
115, Envato Elements Pty Ltd, RantautypeStudio, Vehicle 3D Icon
116, Envato Elements Pty Ltd, PixelSquid360, Body Build Gym Exercise Health
117, Envato Elements Pty Ltd, esysyarof, Fitness 3D Icon
117, Envato Elements Pty Ltd, veeslstudio, Cartoon Cute Boy Doing Workout
118, Envato Elements Pty Ltd, ekatastudio, Cloud Computing 3D Icons
118, Envato Elements Pty Ltd, khurasan, The Cute Fighter
119, Envato Elements Pty Ltd, ekatastudio, Cloud Computing 3D Icons
120, Envato Elements Pty Ltd, PixelSquid360, Body Build Gym Exercise Health
121, Envato Elements Pty Ltd, Dyahcreative, 3D Summer Illustration
121, Envato Elements Pty Ltd, Dyahcreative, 3D Travel & Vacation
121, Envato Elements Pty Ltd, esysyarof, Fitness 3D Icon
121, Envato Elements Pty Ltd, uicreativenet, 3D Weather Objects
122, Envato Elements Pty Ltd, ekatastudio, Cloud Computing 3D Icons
122, Envato Elements Pty Ltd, permadicreative, Safe Box with Money 3D Illustration
123, Envato Elements Pty Ltd, ekatastudio, Cloud Computing 3D Icons
124, Envato Elements Pty Ltd, PixelSquid360, Body Build Gym Exercise Health
126, Envato Elements Pty Ltd, ekatastudio, Cloud Computing 3D Icons
126, Envato Elements Pty Ltd, kit8, Medieval Castle. Tower Building
127, Envato Elements Pty Ltd, ekatastudio, Cloud Computing 3D Icons
129, Envato Elements Pty Ltd, wowomnom, 3D Money Factory
130, Envato Elements Pty Ltd, spacestudios, Banking 3D Icon
132, Envato Elements Pty Ltd, PixelSquid360, Body Build Gym Exercise Health
134, Envato Elements Pty Ltd, slabdsgn, 3d Building Illustration Vol.1
135, Envato Elements Pty Ltd, konkapp, 30 Bill and Payment Icons
135, Envato Elements Pty Ltd, Krafted, 80 Sustainable Living Icons
135, Envato Elements Pty Ltd, Krafted, Industry Icons
135, Envato Elements Pty Ltd, PixelSquid360, Old Boots
138, Envato Elements Pty Ltd, RakataStudio, April Fools Day 3D Illustrations
139, Charles Hodge - IVT Press, Charles Hodge, Fisicality
140, Envato Elements Pty Ltd, PixelSquid360, Body Build Gym Exercise Health
142, Charles Hodge - IVT Press, Charles Hodge, SS Tracker
143, Charles Hodge - IVT Press, Charles Hodge, Net Worth
144, Charles Hodge - IVT Press, Charles Hodge, Razor
146, Envato Elements Pty Ltd, PixelSquid360, Body Build Gym Exercise Health
147, Envato Elements Pty Ltd, esysyarof, Fitness 3D Icon
148, Envato Elements Pty Ltd, graphics4u, Modern 3d illustration of Clipboard with checklist
148, Envato Elements Pty Ltd, Vektorastudio, E-commerce Pack - 3D Illustration
156, Envato Elements Pty Ltd, EklipStudio, Accounting 3D Icon Set
157, Envato Elements Pty Ltd, Faber14, Building Construction Site
158, Envato Elements Pty Ltd, PixelSquid360, Body Build Gym Exercise Health
160, Envato Elements Pty Ltd, AtlasComposer, Concept of business strategy on yellow
162, Envato Elements Pty Ltd, PixelSquid360, Body Build Gym Exercise Health
163, Envato Elements Pty Ltd, Faber14, Summer Landscape
163, Envato Elements Pty Ltd, PixelSquid360, Spoon

165, Envato Elements Pty Ltd, slabdsgn, 3d Building Illustration Vol.1
166, Envato Elements Pty Ltd, ndanko, Texture of black chalk board, place for inscription
167, Envato Elements Pty Ltd, ekatastudio, Investment 3D Icon
167, Envato Elements Pty Ltd, esysyarof, Fitness 3D Icon
167, Envato Elements Pty Ltd, RantautypeStudio, Real Estate 3D Illustration
167, Envato Elements Pty Ltd, Vektorastudio, Design Thinking 3D Illustration
168, Envato Elements Pty Ltd, PixelSquid360, Body Build Gym Exercise Health
169, Envato Elements Pty Ltd, Rexcanor, black Ninja cartoon collection in various
172, Envato Elements Pty Ltd, PixelSquid360, Body Build Gym Exercise Health
173, Envato Elements Pty Ltd, esysyarof, Fitness 3D Icon
173, Envato Elements Pty Ltd, PixelSquid360, Basketball Adult Size
174, Envato Elements Pty Ltd, ekatastudio, Accounting 3D Icons
175, Envato Elements Pty Ltd, TZ78DBM, MIND BLOWN!
176, Envato Elements Pty Ltd, deviap366, Accounting 3D Icon
176, Envato Elements Pty Ltd, ekatastudio, Green Energy 3D Icon
176, Envato Elements Pty Ltd, permadicreative, Accounting 3D Icon
176, Envato Elements Pty Ltd, PixelSquid360, Residential Building Night Glow
176, Envato Elements Pty Ltd, RakataStudio, Smart Security 3D Illustration
177, Envato Elements Pty Ltd, Skyclick2021, Labour Outline Style Icon set
180, Envato Elements Pty Ltd, Xvector, 3D Travel Bag Icon Set
180, Envato Elements Pty Ltd, Xvector, 3D Travel Bag Icon Set
186, Envato Elements Pty Ltd, PixelSquid360, Dark Money Icon
186, Envato Elements Pty Ltd, PixelSquid360, Moonshine Apparatus
190, Envato Elements Pty Ltd, PixelSquid360, Dumbbell
190, Envato Elements Pty Ltd, PixelSquid360, Moonshine Apparatus
212, Envato Elements Pty Ltd, Icons8, Design Thinking and Creative Idea
Cover, Charles Hodge - IVT Press, Charles Hodge, CHODGE Logo
Cover, Envato Elements Pty Ltd, veeslstudio, Cartoon Cute Boy Doing Workout

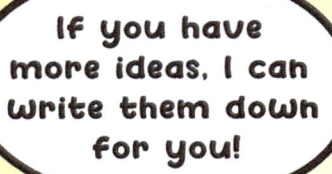

COMING UP NEXT TIME!
ON THE FISICALITY FILES

"THE CENTURY SOLUTION:
The 100-Year Planning Cycle for
Building Generational Wealth"

www.ingramcontent.com/pod-product-compliance
Lightning Source LLC
Chambersburg PA
CBHW051145120626
46547CB00012B/949